Ivan Kushnir

Economy of Brunei

Series "Economy in countries"

first published: 2019
last updated: 2021-01-26

Ivan Kushnir. Economy of Brunei. Series "Economy in countries". - 2019. - 69 pages.

This book about the economy of Brunei from the 1970s to the 2010s. Source data from UN Data.

Size. In the 2010s, the gross domestic product of Brunei was equal to $15.0 billion per year; the value of agriculture was $128.5 million; the value of industry was $9.6 billion. Since the share in the world is between .01% and .1%, the country is classified as a small economy.

Productivity. In the 2010s, the GDP per capita was $36 427.0, the value of agriculture per capita was $312.2, the value of industry per capita was $23 432.4. Since the productivity is greater the average above average, the economy is classified as high developed.

Growth. In the 2010s, the growth of GDP was 0.47%; the growth of agriculture was 0.039%; the growth of industry was -0.70%.

Structure. In the 2010s, the economy of Brunei consisted of: industry (63.3%), services (25.1%), trade (5.2%), transportation (3.3%), construction (2.2%), and agriculture (0.84%).

Exports and imports. In the 2010s, the exports were 66.2% higher than the imports, the net exports were equal to 24.6% of the GDP. The technological structure of exports are not better than the structure of imports.

Consumption and reproduction. The attitude of reproduction to the consumption is not better than the global average, so the share of GDP in the world will not increase.

Series "Economy in countries": parallel.page.link/en

ISBN: 9781794660298

Contents

Part I. Size

	The 2010s
GDP	$15.0 billion
The share in the world	0.019%
Share in Asia	0.055%
Share in South-Eastern Asia	0.58%

Chapter I. Gross domestic product

The gross domestic product of Brunei grew from $1.4 billion per year in the 1970s to $15.0 billion per year in the 2010s, that is by $13.6 billion or 10.6 times. The change occurred at $12.7 billion due to a 6.5-fold increase in prices, as also at -$1.4 billion due to a 1.6-fold decrease in productivity, as well as at $2.3 billion due to the growth in population. The average annual growth in gross domestic product is 2.0%. The minimum value of GDP was in 1970 at $224.9 million. The maximum value of gross domestic product was in 2012 at $19.0 billion.

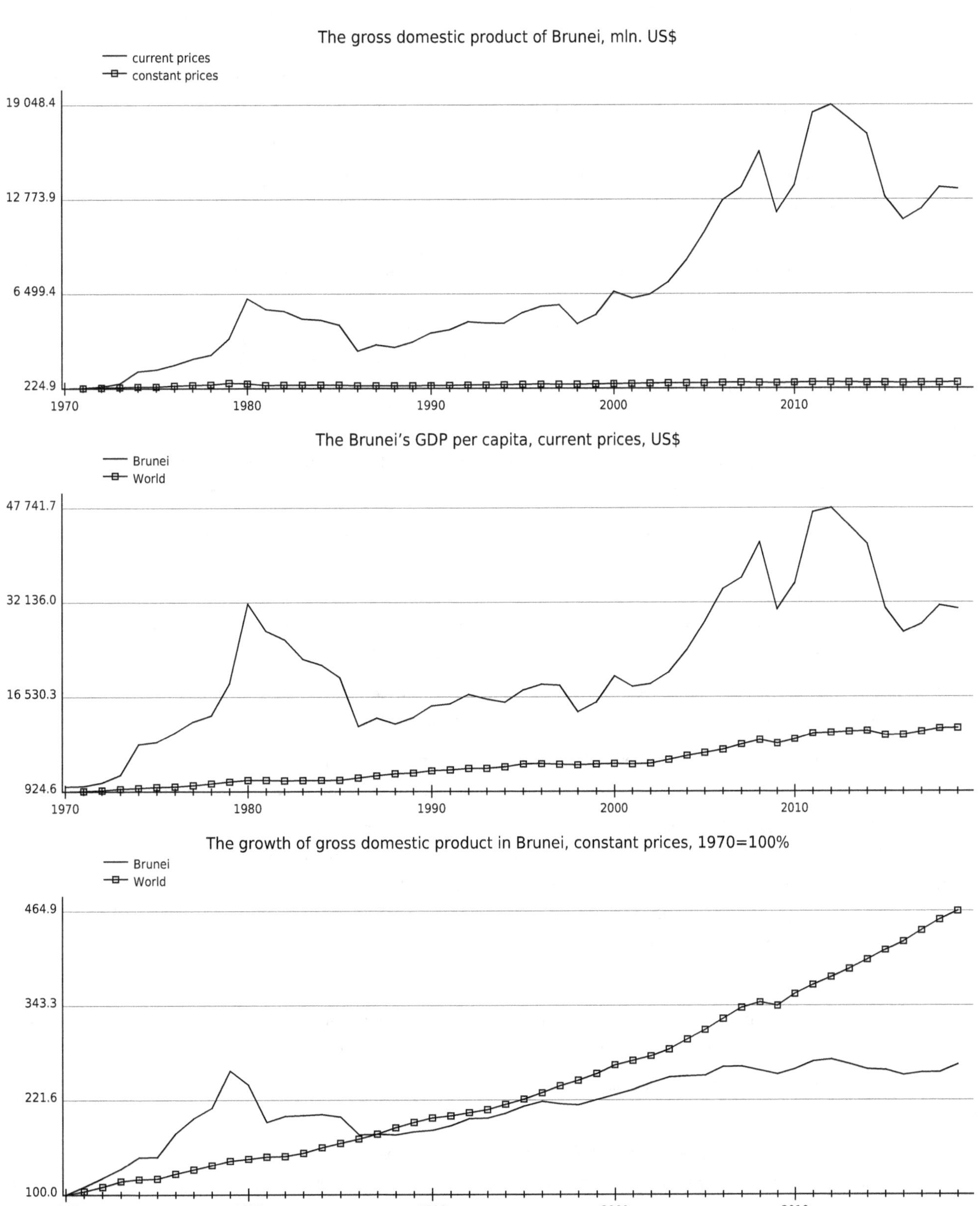

The 1970s

The Brunei's gross domestic product was $1.4 billion per year in the 1970s, ranked 106th in the world, and was on a par with Nepal ($1.4 billion), Bahrain ($1.4 billion). The share in the world was 0.022%, and 0.12% in Asia.

The gross domestic product of Brunei included: government expenditure (10.1%), household expenditure (9.0%), capital formation (4.4%), and net export (76.6%).

The Brunei's GDP per capita was $8 898.6 in the 1970s, ranked 9th in the world. The gross domestic product per capita in Brunei was greater than GDP per capita in the world ($1 620.8) in 5.5 times, and was greater than gross domestic product per capita in Asia ($525.2) in 16.9 times.

The growth of GDP in Brunei was 11.2% in the 1970s, ranked 6th in the world, and was on a par with Saudi Arabia (11.2%). The growth of gross domestic product in Brunei (11.2%) was greater than growth of GDP in the world (4.1%), was greater than growth of gross domestic product in Asia (5.5%).

Comparison with neighbors. The gross domestic product of Brunei was less than in Malaysia ($10.1 billion). The gross domestic product per capita in Brunei was greater than in Malaysia ($840.6). The growth of gross domestic product in Brunei was greater than in Malaysia (9.7%).

Comparison with leaders. The Brunei's gross domestic product was less than in the United States ($1.7 trillion), in the USSR ($649.4 billion), in Japan ($558.0 billion), in Germany ($484.2 billion), and in France ($333.2 billion). The gross domestic product per capita in Brunei was greater than in the United States ($7.8 thousand), in France ($6.2 thousand), in Germany ($6.1 thousand), in Japan ($5.0 thousand), and in the USSR ($2.6 thousand). The growth of GDP in Brunei was greater than in the USSR (4.8%), in Japan (4.6%), in France (3.9%), in the USA (3.5%), and in Germany (3.1%).

The 1980s

The Brunei's gross domestic product was $4.3 billion per year in the 1980s, ranked 94th in the world, and was on a par with Honduras ($4.3 billion), Bahrain ($4.3 billion), Papua New Guinea ($4.4 billion). The share in the world was 0.029%, and 0.12% in Asia.

The GDP of Brunei consisted of: public expenditure (14.6%), capital formation (12.6%), household expenditure (10.2%), and net export (58.3%).

The GDP per capita in Brunei was $19 419.1 in the 1980s, ranked 7th in the world, and was on a par with Qatar ($19.1 thousand). The gross domestic product per capita in Brunei was greater than gross domestic product per capita in the world ($3 123.4) in 6.2 times, and was greater than gross domestic product per capita in Asia ($1 222.0) in 15.9 times.

The growth of gross domestic product in Brunei was -3.5% in the 1980s, ranked 183rd in the world. The growth of GDP in Brunei (-3.5%) was less than growth of GDP in the world (3.0%), was less than growth of GDP in Asia (4.6%).

Comparison with neighbors. The gross domestic product of Brunei was less than in Malaysia ($30.6 billion). The GDP per capita in Brunei was greater than in Malaysia ($1 971.3). The growth of gross domestic product in Brunei was less than in Malaysia (5.7%).

Comparison with leaders. The Brunei's gross domestic product was less than in the USA ($4.2 trillion), in Japan ($1.8 trillion), in Germany ($990.0 billion), in the USSR ($887.0 billion), and in France ($729.5 billion). The GDP per capita in Brunei was greater than in the United States ($17.4 thousand), in Japan ($15.0 thousand), in France ($12.9 thousand), in Germany ($12.7 thousand), and in the USSR ($3.2 thousand). The growth of GDP in Brunei was less than in the USSR (4.3%), in Japan (4.3%), in the United States (3.1%), in France (2.3%), and in Germany (1.9%).

The 1990s

The GDP of Brunei was $4.8 billion per year in the 1990s, ranked 114th in the world, and was on a par with Honduras ($4.8 billion), Guinea ($4.7 billion), Estonia ($4.9 billion). The share in the world was 0.017%, and 0.062% in Asia.

The GDP of Brunei consisted of: capital formation (44.2%), government expenditure (25.4%), household expenditure (22.5%), and net export (3.9%).

The GDP per capita in Brunei was $16 378.5 in the 1990s, ranked 37th in the world, and was on a par with New Caledonia ($16.7 thousand). The Brunei's GDP per capita was greater than gross domestic product per capita in the world ($5 020.1) in 3.3 times, and was greater than gross domestic product per capita in Asia ($2 243.8) in 7.3 times.

The growth of gross domestic product in Brunei was 2.1% in the 1990s, ranked 131st in the world, and was on a par with Greece (2.0%), Zimbabwe (2.0%), the FSM (2.1%). The growth of GDP in Brunei (2.1%) was less than growth of gross domestic product in the world (2.8%), was less than growth of GDP in Asia (4.7%).

Comparison with neighbors. The Brunei's gross domestic product was less than in Malaysia ($73.5 billion). The Brunei's gross domestic product per capita was greater than in Malaysia ($3.6 thousand). The growth of gross domestic product in Brunei was less than in Malaysia (7.1%).

Comparison with leaders. The Brunei's GDP was less than in the USA ($7.6 trillion), in Japan ($4.3 trillion), in Germany ($2.2 trillion), in France ($1.4 trillion), and in the UK ($1.3 trillion). The Brunei's gross domestic product per capita was less than in Japan ($34.3 thousand), in the USA ($28.7 thousand), in Germany ($27.0 thousand), in France ($24.1 thousand), and in the UK ($22.9 thousand). The growth of GDP in Brunei was greater than in France (2.0%) and in Japan (1.5%); but less than in the United States (3.2%), in the UK (2.3%), and in Germany (2.2%).

The 2000s

The GDP of Brunei was $10.0 billion per year in the 2000s, ranked 114th in the world, and was on a par with Honduras ($10.1 billion). The share in the world was 0.021%, and 0.080% in Asia.

The gross domestic product of Brunei included: government expenditure (21.5%), capital formation (20.8%), household consumption expenditure (14.3%), and net export (32.1%).

The Brunei's gross domestic product per capita was $27 729.3 in the 2000s, ranked 33rd in the world, and was on a par with Hong Kong ($27.5 thousand). The GDP per capita in Brunei was greater than gross domestic product per capita in the world ($7 176.3) in 3.9 times, and was greater than GDP per capita in Asia ($3 180.5) in 8.7 times.

The growth of gross domestic product in Brunei was 1.4% in the 2000s, ranked 179th in the world, and was on a par with San Marino (1.4%), French Polynesia (1.4%). The growth of gross domestic product in Brunei (1.4%) was less than growth of gross domestic product in the world (3.0%), was less than growth of gross domestic product in Asia (5.2%).

Comparison with neighbors. The Brunei's gross domestic product was less than in Malaysia ($145.5 billion). The gross domestic product per capita in Brunei was greater than in Malaysia ($5.7 thousand). The growth of gross domestic product in Brunei was less than in Malaysia (4.7%).

Comparison with leaders. The GDP of Brunei was less than in the United States ($12.6 trillion), in Japan ($4.7 trillion), in Germany ($2.8 trillion), in China ($2.6 trillion), and in the UK ($2.3 trillion). The Brunei's gross domestic product per capita was greater than in China ($1 954.1); but less than in the USA ($42.8 thousand), in the UK ($38.4 thousand), in Japan ($36.4 thousand), and in Germany ($34.0 thousand). The growth of GDP in Brunei was greater than in Germany (0.73%) and in Japan (0.50%); but less than in China (10.3%), in the United States (1.9%), and in the United Kingdom (1.7%).

The 2010s

The Brunei's GDP was $15.0 billion per year in the 2010s, ranked 123rd in the world, and was on a par with Mozambique ($14.8 billion). The share in the world was 0.019%, and 0.055% in Asia.

The GDP of Brunei included: capital formation (33.1%), public expenditure (22.3%), household expenditure (16.9%), and net export (24.6%).

The gross domestic product per capita in Brunei was $36 427.0 in the 2010s, ranked 35th in the world, and was on a par with New Caledonia ($36.2 thousand). The Brunei's GDP per capita was greater than GDP per capita in the world ($10 603.1) in 3.4 times, and was greater than GDP per capita in Asia ($6 207.1) in 5.9 times.

The growth of gross domestic product in Brunei was 0.5% in the 2010s, ranked 188th in the world. The growth of GDP in Brunei (0.47%) was less than growth of gross domestic product in the world (3.1%), was less than growth of gross domestic product in Asia (5.2%).

Comparison with neighbors. The GDP of Brunei was 21.2 times lower than in Malaysia ($317.4 billion). The Brunei's gross domestic product per capita was 3.5 times higher than in Malaysia ($10.6 thousand). The growth of gross domestic product in Brunei was less than in Malaysia (5.3%).

Comparison with leaders. The Brunei's GDP was 1 197.7 times lower than in the United States ($18.0 trillion), 700.6 times lower than in

China ($10.5 trillion), 348.6 times lower than in Japan ($5.2 trillion), 244.2 times lower than in Germany ($3.7 trillion), and 184.5 times lower than in the United Kingdom ($2.8 trillion). The Brunei's gross domestic product per capita was 4.9 times higher than in China ($7.5 thousand); but 35.2% lower than in the USA ($56.2 thousand), 18.6% lower than in Germany ($44.7 thousand), 13.6% lower than in the UK ($42.2 thousand), and 10.9% lower than in Japan ($40.9 thousand). The growth of GDP in Brunei was less than in China (7.7%), in the United States (2.3%), in Germany (1.9%), in the United Kingdom (1.8%), and in Japan (1.3%).

Chapter II. Value added

The value added of Brunei enlarged from $1.5 billion per year in the 1970s to $15.3 billion per year in the 2010s, that is by $13.8 billion or 10.4 times. The change occurred at $13.1 billion due to a 7.0-fold increase in prices, as also at -$1.6 billion due to a 1.7-fold decrease in productivity, as well as at $2.3 billion due to the rise in population. The average annual growth in value added is 1.7%. The minimum value of value added was in 1970 at $224.9 million. The maximum value of value added was in 2012 at $19.4 billion.

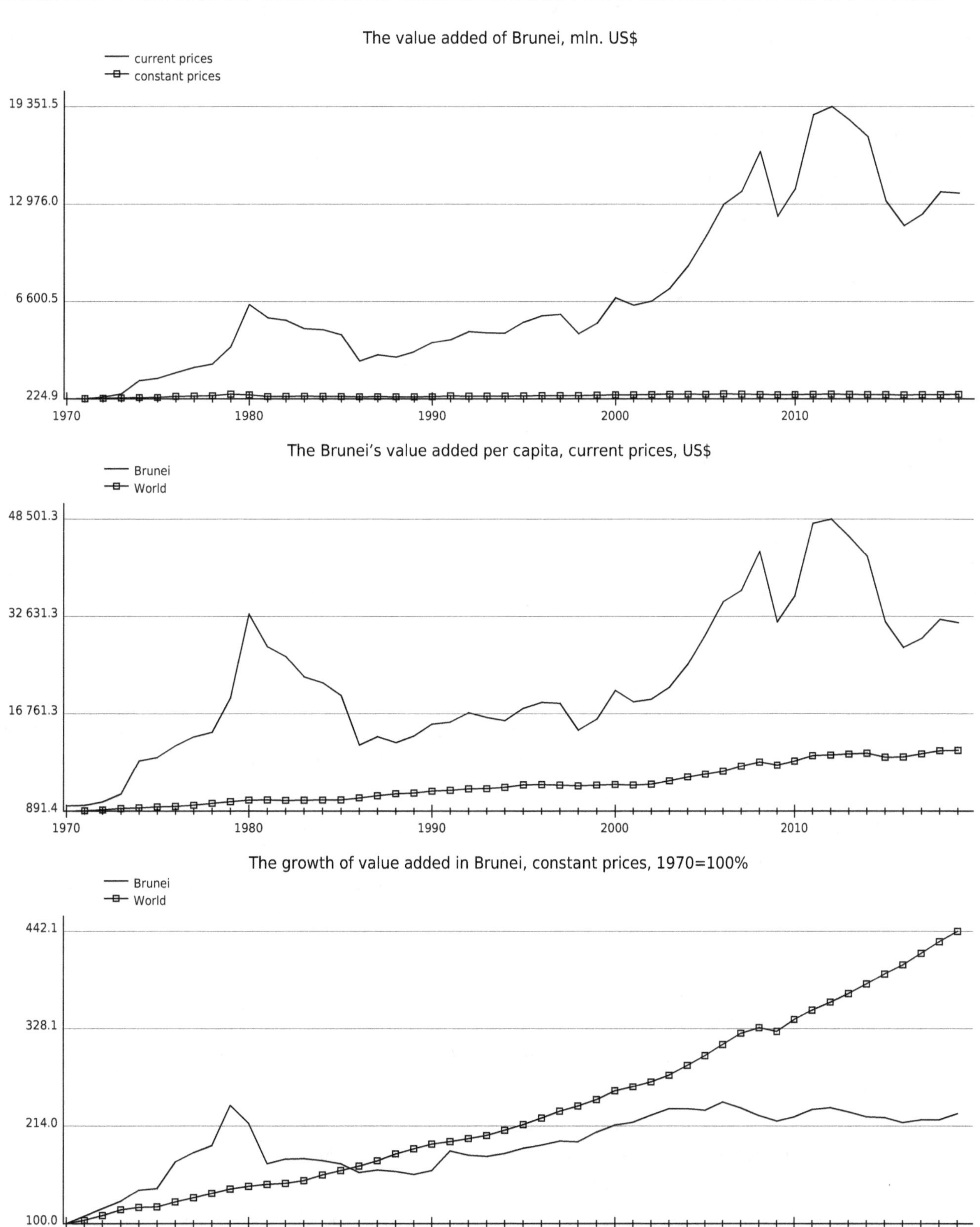

The 1970s

The value added of Brunei was $1.5 billion per year in the 1970s, ranked 104th in the world, and was on a par with Honduras ($1.5 billion). The share in the world was 0.023%, and 0.12% in Asia.

The total value added of Brunei consisted of: industry (89.5%), services (6.6%), trade (2.3%), construction (0.68%), transportation (0.63%), and agriculture (0.35%).

The Brunei's value added per capita was $9 256.4 in the 1970s, ranked 7th in the world. The value added per capita in Brunei was greater than value added per capita in the world ($1 564.4) in 5.9 times, and was greater than value added per capita in Asia ($508.3) in 18.2 times.

The growth of value added in Brunei was 10.1% in the 1970s, ranked 8th in the world. The growth of value added in Brunei (10.1%) was greater than growth of value added in the world (3.9%), was greater than growth of value added in Asia (5.5%).

Comparison with neighbors. The value added of Brunei was less than in Malaysia ($10.0 billion). The value added per capita in Brunei was greater than in Malaysia ($832.5). The growth of value added in Brunei was greater than in Malaysia (8.8%).

Comparison with leaders. The Brunei's value added was less than in the United States ($1.7 trillion), in the USSR ($649.4 billion), in Japan ($545.3 billion), in Germany ($444.9 billion), and in France ($297.3 billion). The value added per capita in Brunei was greater than in the USA ($7.8 thousand), in Germany ($5.7 thousand), in France ($5.5 thousand), in Japan ($4.9 thousand), and in the USSR ($2.6 thousand). The growth of value added in Brunei was greater than in Japan (4.9%), in the USSR (4.8%), in France (3.7%), in Germany (3.1%), and in the USA (2.9%).

The 1980s

The value added of Brunei was $4.3 billion per year in the 1980s, ranked 95th in the world, and was on a par with Gabon ($4.3 billion), Senegal ($4.4 billion), Honduras ($4.2 billion). The share in the world was 0.030%, and 0.13% in Asia.

The total value added of Brunei included: industry (78.1%), services (14.1%), trade (4.7%), transportation (1.6%), construction (1.1%), and agriculture (0.44%).

The Brunei's value added per capita was $19 541.6 in the 1980s, ranked 7th in the world. The Brunei's value added per capita was greater than value added per capita in the world ($3 029.9) in 6.4 times, and was greater than value added per capita in Asia ($1 191.9) in 16.4 times.

The growth of value added in Brunei was -4% in the 1980s, ranked 182nd in the world. The growth of value added in Brunei (-4.0%) was less than growth of value added in the world (2.9%), was less than growth of value added in Asia (4.3%).

Comparison with neighbors. The value added of Brunei was less than in Malaysia ($30.7 billion). The value added per capita in Brunei was greater than in Malaysia ($1 976.4). The growth of value added in Brunei was less than in Malaysia (5.6%).

Comparison with leaders. The value added of Brunei was less than in the United States ($4.2 trillion), in Japan ($1.8 trillion), in Germany ($907.0 billion), in the USSR ($887.0 billion), and in France ($650.9 billion). The value added per capita in Brunei was greater than in the United States ($17.4 thousand), in Japan ($14.8 thousand), in Germany ($11.6 thousand), in France ($11.5 thousand), and in the USSR ($3.2 thousand). The growth of value added in Brunei was less than in the USSR (4.3%), in Japan (4.2%), in the United States (2.8%), in France (2.2%), and in Germany (2.0%).

The 1990s

The value added of Brunei was $4.8 billion per year in the 1990s, ranked 114th in the world, and was on a par with Macao ($4.9 billion). The share in the world was 0.018%, and 0.063% in Asia.

The total value added of Brunei included: industry (52.8%), services (31.5%), trade (6.3%), transportation (4.3%), construction (3.9%), and agriculture (1.1%).

The Brunei's value added per capita was $16 410.1 in the 1990s, ranked 35th in the world, and was on a par with New Caledonia ($16.3 thousand). The Brunei's value added per capita was greater than value added per capita in the world ($4 799.9) in 3.4 times, and was greater than value added per capita in Asia ($2 197.3) in 7.5 times.

The growth of value added in Brunei was 2.8% in the 1990s, ranked 105th in the world, and was on a par with the Americas (2.8%). The growth of value added in Brunei (2.8%) was greater than growth of value added in the world (2.7%), was less than growth of value added in Asia (4.6%).

Comparison with neighbors. The value added of Brunei was less than in Malaysia ($75.7 billion). The Brunei's value added per capita was greater than in Malaysia ($3.7 thousand). The growth of value added in Brunei was less than in Malaysia (6.6%).

Comparison with leaders. The value added of Brunei was less than in the USA ($7.6 trillion), in Japan ($4.3 trillion), in Germany ($2.0 trillion), in France ($1.3 trillion), and in the UK ($1.2 trillion). The Brunei's value added per capita was less than in Japan ($34.2 thousand), in the United States ($28.6 thousand), in Germany ($24.5 thousand), in France ($21.6 thousand), and in the UK ($21.4 thousand). The growth of value added in Brunei was greater than in the UK (2.4%), in Germany (2.1%), in France (1.8%), and in Japan (1.8%); but less than in the United States (2.8%).

The 2000s

The Brunei's value added was $10.2 billion per year in the 2000s, ranked 108th in the world, and was on a par with Senegal ($10.1 billion), Jamaica ($10.0 billion). The share in the world was 0.023%, and 0.083% in Asia.

The total value added of Brunei included: industry (67.4%), services (23.0%), trade (4.2%), transportation (2.8%), construction (1.7%), and agriculture (0.84%).

The Brunei's value added per capita was $28 382.6 in the 2000s, ranked 31st in the world. The value added per capita in Brunei was greater than value added per capita in the world ($6 818.0) in 4.2 times, and was greater than value added per capita in Asia ($3 111.3) in 9.1 times.

The growth of value added in Brunei was 0.6% in the 2000s, ranked 196th in the world. The growth of value added in Brunei (0.62%) was less than growth of value added in the world (2.9%), was less than growth of value added in Asia (5.1%).

Comparison with neighbors. The value added of Brunei was less than in Malaysia ($146.1 billion). The value added per capita in Brunei was greater than in Malaysia ($5.7 thousand). The growth of value added in Brunei was less than in Malaysia (4.4%).

Comparison with leaders. The value added of Brunei was less than in the USA ($12.6 trillion), in Japan ($4.7 trillion), in China ($2.6 trillion), in Germany ($2.5 trillion), and in the UK ($2.1 trillion). The Brunei's value added per capita was greater than in China ($1 954.1); but less than in the USA ($42.8 thousand), in Japan ($36.4 thousand), in the United Kingdom ($34.6 thousand), and in Germany ($30.7 thousand). The growth of value added in Brunei was greater than in Japan (0.27%); but less than in China (10.2%), in the United States (1.7%), in the United Kingdom (1.7%), and in Germany (0.65%).

The 2010s

The value added of Brunei was $15.3 billion per year in the 2010s, ranked 120th in the world, and was on a par with Gabon ($15.2 billion), Bosnia and Herzegovina ($15.4 billion). The share in the world was 0.021%, and 0.057% in Asia.

The total value added of Brunei included: industry (63.3%), services (25.1%), trade (5.2%), transportation (3.3%), construction (2.2%), and agriculture (0.84%).

The Brunei's value added per capita was $37 042.5 in the 2010s, ranked 32nd in the world, and was on a par with New Zealand ($37.3 thousand), the UK ($37.7 thousand), France ($36.2 thousand). The value added per capita in Brunei was greater than value added per capita in the world ($10 094.6) in 3.7 times, and was greater than value added per capita in Asia ($6 065.5) in 6.1 times.

The growth of value added in Brunei was 0.4% in the 2010s, ranked 189th in the world. The growth of value added in Brunei (0.38%) was less than growth of value added in the world (3.1%), was less than growth of value added in Asia (5.3%).

Comparison with neighbors. The Brunei's value added was 20.6 times lower than in Malaysia ($313.9 billion). The value added per capita in Brunei was 3.6 times higher than in Malaysia ($10.4 thousand). The growth of value added in Brunei was less than in Malaysia (5.3%).

Comparison with leaders. The value added of Brunei was 1 177.8 times lower than in the United States ($18.0 trillion), 688.9 times lower than in China ($10.5 trillion), 341.1 times lower than in Japan ($5.2 trillion), 216.6 times lower than in Germany ($3.3 trillion), and 162.0 times lower than in the United Kingdom ($2.5 trillion). The Brunei's value added per capita was 4.9 times higher than in China ($7.5 thousand); but 34.1% lower than in the United States ($56.2 thousand), 8.9% lower than in Japan ($40.7 thousand), 8.2% lower than in Germany ($40.3 thousand), and 1.6% lower than in the UK ($37.7 thousand). The growth of value added in Brunei was less than in China (7.7%), in the USA (2.2%), in Germany (1.9%), in the UK (1.8%), and in Japan (1.3%).

Chapter III. Gross national income

The gross national income of Brunei increased from $1.4 billion per year in the 1970s to $15.0 billion per year in the 2010s, that is by $13.6 billion or 10.7 times. The change occurred at $12.7 billion due to a 6.5-fold increase in prices, as also at -$1.3 billion due to a 1.6-fold decrease in productivity, as well as at $2.3 billion due to the increase in population. The average annual growth in GNI is 2.0%. The minimum value of GNI was in 1970 at $224.9 million. The maximum value of GNI was in 2012 at $18.6 billion.

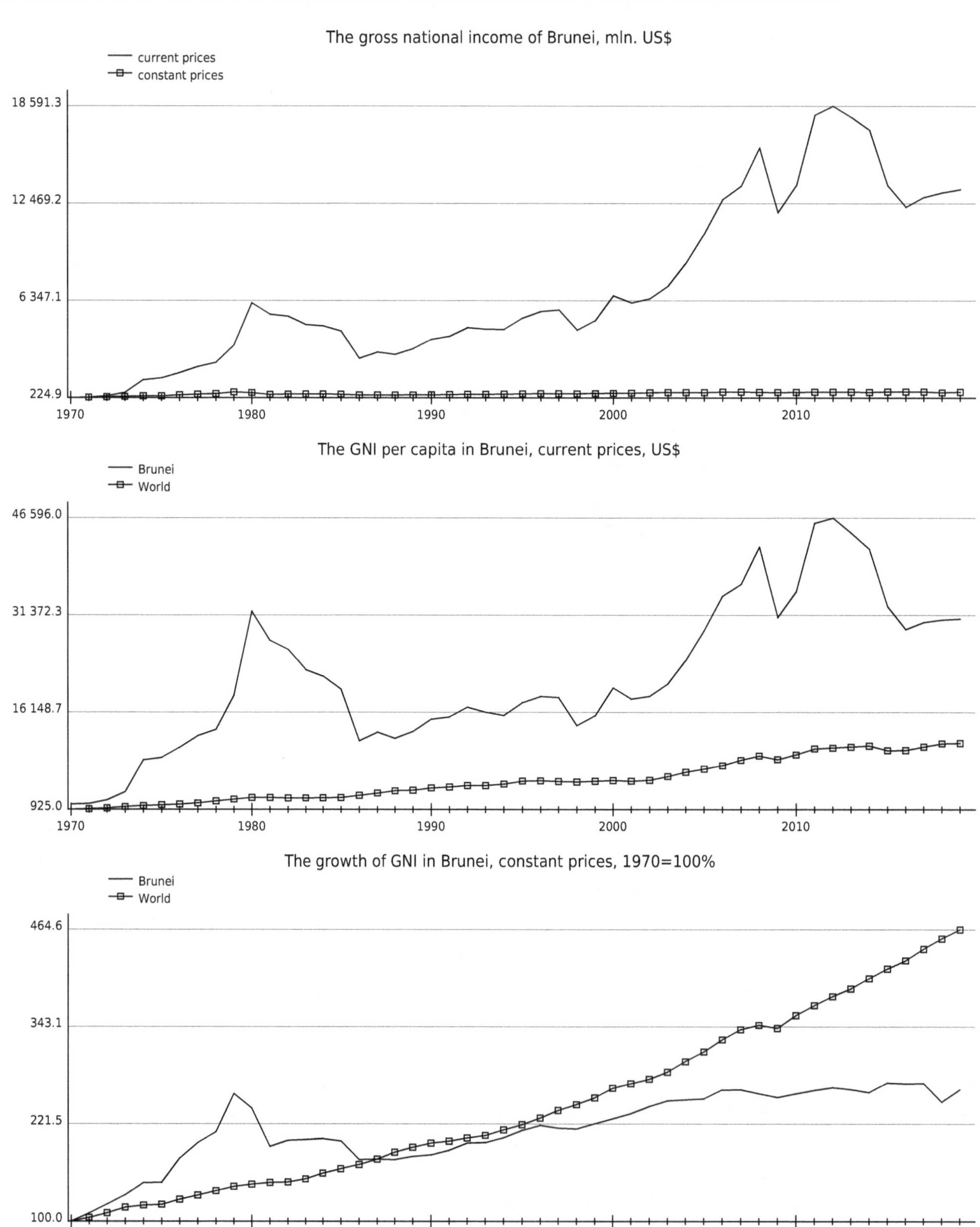

The 1970s

The GNI of Brunei was $1.4 billion per year in the 1970s, ranked 108th in the world, and was on a par with Nepal ($1.4 billion), Honduras ($1.4 billion). The share in the world was 0.021%, and 0.11% in Asia.

The Brunei's GNI per capita was $8 898.6 in the 1970s, ranked 9th in the world, and was on a par with Sweden ($9.0 thousand). The Brunei's GNI per capita was greater than GNI per capita in the world ($1 624.3) in 5.5 times, and was greater than GNI per capita in Asia ($529.4) in 16.8 times.

The growth of gross national income in Brunei was 11.2% in the 1970s, ranked 6th in the world. The growth of GNI in Brunei (11.2%) was greater than growth of GNI in the world (4.1%), was greater than growth of GNI in Asia (5.5%).

Comparison with neighbors. The Brunei's GNI was less than in Malaysia ($9.7 billion). The Brunei's GNI per capita was greater than in Malaysia ($808.0). The growth of GNI in Brunei was greater than in Malaysia (9.3%).

Comparison with leaders. The GNI of Brunei was less than in the United States ($1.7 trillion), in the USSR ($649.4 billion), in Japan ($558.5 billion), in Germany ($486.2 billion), and in France ($334.3 billion). The Brunei's gross national income per capita was greater than in the United States ($7.8 thousand), in France ($6.2 thousand), in Germany ($6.2 thousand), in Japan ($5.0 thousand), and in the USSR ($2.6 thousand). The growth of GNI in Brunei was greater than in the USSR (4.8%), in Japan (4.7%), in France (3.9%), in the United States (3.5%), and in Germany (3.0%).

The 1980s

The Brunei's GNI was $4.3 billion per year in the 1980s, ranked 93rd in the world, and was on a par with Gabon ($4.2 billion), Senegal ($4.4 billion). The share in the world was 0.029%, and 0.12% in Asia.

The GNI per capita in Brunei was $19 419.1 in the 1980s, ranked 8th in the world. The gross national income per capita in Brunei was greater than gross national income per capita in the world ($3 117.1) in 6.2 times, and was greater than gross national income per capita in Asia ($1 233.8) in 15.7 times.

The growth of GNI in Brunei was -3.5% in the 1980s, ranked 182nd in the world. The growth of gross national income in Brunei (-3.5%) was less than growth of GNI in the world (3.0%), was less than growth of GNI in Asia (4.6%).

Comparison with neighbors. The Brunei's gross national income was less than in Malaysia ($28.8 billion). The Brunei's gross national income per capita was greater than in Malaysia ($1 859.5). The growth of GNI in Brunei was less than in Malaysia (5.6%).

Comparison with leaders. The Brunei's gross national income was less than in the USA ($4.2 trillion), in Japan ($1.8 trillion), in Germany ($996.5 billion), in the USSR ($887.0 billion), and in France ($732.1 billion). The gross national income per capita in Brunei was greater than in the USA ($17.4 thousand), in Japan ($15.0 thousand), in France ($13.0 thousand), in Germany ($12.8 thousand), and in the USSR ($3.2 thousand). The growth of gross national income in Brunei was less than in Japan (4.4%), in the USSR (4.3%), in the USA (3.1%), in France (2.3%), and in Germany (2.0%).

The 1990s

The gross national income of Brunei was $4.8 billion per year in the 1990s, ranked 114th in the world, and was on a par with Gabon ($4.9 billion), Estonia ($4.9 billion). The share in the world was 0.017%, and 0.061% in Asia.

The GNI per capita in Brunei was $16 378.5 in the 1990s, ranked 37th in the world, and was on a par with Macao ($16.2 thousand), Kuwait ($16.2 thousand), New Caledonia ($16.7 thousand). The Brunei's GNI per capita was greater than GNI per capita in the world ($4 991.4) in 3.3 times, and was greater than GNI per capita in Asia ($2 257.5) in 7.3 times.

The growth of GNI in Brunei was 2.1% in the 1990s, ranked 132nd in the world. The growth of gross national income in Brunei (2.1%) was less than growth of gross national income in the world (2.8%), was less than growth of gross national income in Asia (4.6%).

Comparison with neighbors. The Brunei's GNI was less than in Malaysia ($69.7 billion). The Brunei's GNI per capita was greater than in Malaysia ($3.4 thousand). The growth of GNI in Brunei was less than in Malaysia (7.0%).

Comparison with leaders. The Brunei's GNI was less than in the USA ($7.5 trillion), in Japan ($4.4 trillion), in Germany ($2.2 trillion), in France ($1.4 trillion), and in the United Kingdom ($1.3 trillion). The Brunei's GNI per capita was less than in Japan ($34.7 thousand), in the USA ($28.5 thousand), in Germany ($27.0 thousand), in France ($24.3 thousand), and in the UK ($23.0 thousand). The growth of gross national income in Brunei was greater than in the UK (2.0%), in Germany (2.0%), and in Japan (1.5%); but less than in the

United States (3.4%) and in France (2.2%).

The 2000s

The GNI of Brunei was $10.0 billion per year in the 2000s, ranked 113th in the world, and was on a par with Honduras ($9.8 billion). The share in the world was 0.021%, and 0.079% in Asia.

The GNI per capita in Brunei was $27 729.3 in the 2000s, ranked 34th in the world, and was on a par with Hong Kong ($28.1 thousand). The gross national income per capita in Brunei was greater than GNI per capita in the world ($7 165.2) in 3.9 times, and was greater than GNI per capita in Asia ($3 199.2) in 8.7 times.

The growth of GNI in Brunei was 1.4% in the 2000s, ranked 179th in the world, and was on a par with French Polynesia (1.4%), Southern Europe (1.4%). The growth of gross national income in Brunei (1.4%) was less than growth of gross national income in the world (3.0%), was less than growth of GNI in Asia (5.3%).

Comparison with neighbors. The GNI of Brunei was less than in Malaysia ($139.6 billion). The Brunei's GNI per capita was greater than in Malaysia ($5.5 thousand). The growth of gross national income in Brunei was less than in Malaysia (5.3%).

Comparison with leaders. The Brunei's gross national income was less than in the USA ($12.7 trillion), in Japan ($4.8 trillion), in Germany ($2.8 trillion), in China ($2.6 trillion), and in the UK ($2.3 trillion). The gross national income per capita in Brunei was greater than in China ($1 950.5); but less than in the United States ($43.2 thousand), in the UK ($38.5 thousand), in Japan ($37.1 thousand), and in Germany ($34.2 thousand). The growth of GNI in Brunei was greater than in Germany (1.0%) and in Japan (0.62%); but less than in China (10.4%), in the USA (1.8%), and in the UK (1.7%).

The 2010s

The gross national income of Brunei was $15.0 billion per year in the 2010s, ranked 121st in the world, and was on a par with Botswana ($15.0 billion), Gabon ($14.8 billion). The share in the world was 0.019%, and 0.055% in Asia.

The Brunei's GNI per capita was $36 520.4 in the 2010s, ranked 34th in the world, and was on a par with New Caledonia ($36.2 thousand), the British Virgin Islands ($35.7 thousand). The Brunei's GNI per capita was greater than GNI per capita in the world ($10 611.7) in 3.4 times, and was greater than gross national income per capita in Asia ($6 227.9) in 5.9 times.

The growth of gross national income in Brunei was 0.4% in the 2010s, ranked 189th in the world. The growth of gross national income in Brunei (0.38%) was less than growth of GNI in the world (3.1%), was less than growth of GNI in Asia (5.2%).

Comparison with neighbors. The Brunei's gross national income was 20.5 times lower than in Malaysia ($307.9 billion). The Brunei's GNI per capita was 3.6 times higher than in Malaysia ($10.2 thousand). The growth of GNI in Brunei was less than in Malaysia (5.3%).

Comparison with leaders. The Brunei's gross national income was 1 217.6 times lower than in the USA ($18.3 trillion), 696.2 times lower than in China ($10.5 trillion), 359.1 times lower than in Japan ($5.4 trillion), 249.4 times lower than in Germany ($3.7 trillion), and 182.6 times lower than in France ($2.7 trillion). The Brunei's gross national income per capita was 4.9 times higher than in China ($7.5 thousand); but 36.3% lower than in the USA ($57.3 thousand), 20.3% lower than in Germany ($45.8 thousand), 13.5% lower than in Japan ($42.2 thousand), and 11.8% lower than in France ($41.4 thousand). The growth of GNI in Brunei was less than in China (7.7%), in the USA (2.5%), in Germany (2.0%), in Japan (1.4%), and in France (1.4%).

Part II. Structure

	The 2010s
agriculture	0.84%
industry	63.3%
construction	2.2%
trade	5.2%
transportation	3.3%
services	25.1%

Chapter IV. Agriculture

Agriculture, hunting, forestry, fishing (ISIC A-B)

The value added of agriculture in Brunei grew up from $5.2 million per year in the 1970s to $128.5 million per year in the 2010s, that is by $123.4 million or 24.8 times. The change occurred at $112.2 million due to a 7.8-fold increase in prices, as also at $2.9 million due to a 1.2-fold increase in productivity, as well as at $8.3 million due to the growth in population. The average annual growth in agriculture is 2.4%. The minimum value of agriculture was in 1970 at $925.5 thousand. The maximum value of agriculture was in 2014 at $147.5 million.

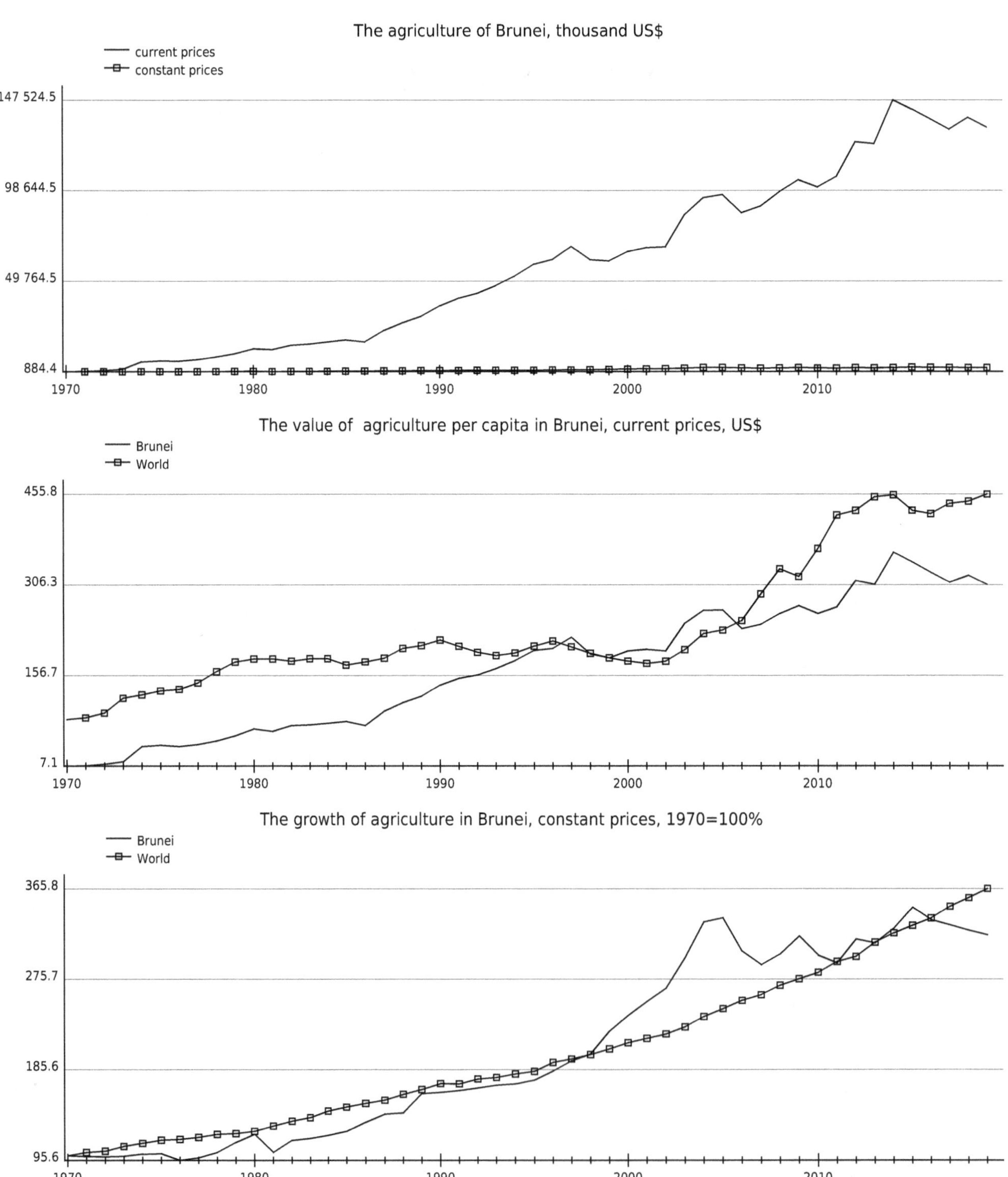

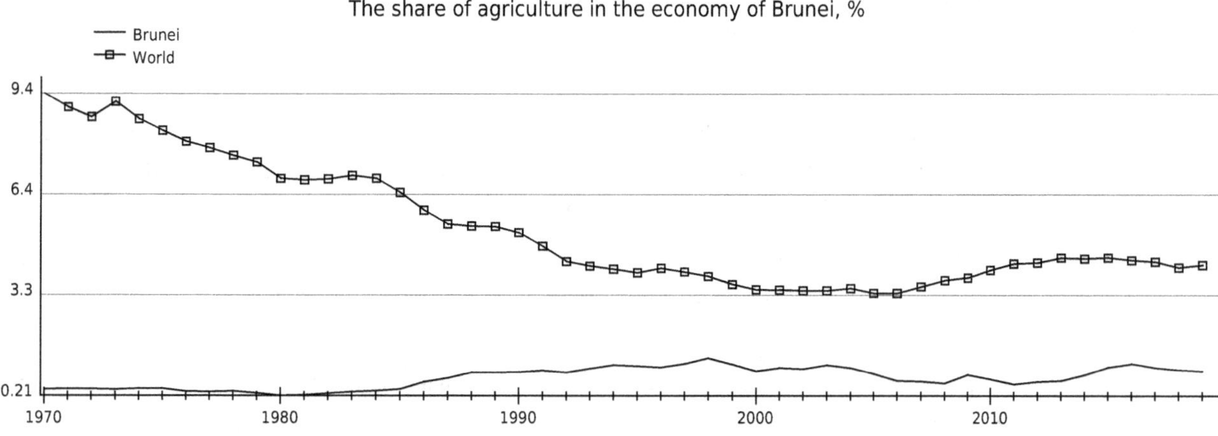

The 1970s

The Brunei's agriculture was $5.2 million per year in the 1970s, ranked 164th in the world. The share in the world was 0.0010%, and 0.0029% in Asia.

The share of agriculture in the economy of Brunei was 0.35% in the 1970s, ranked 179th in the world.

The value of agriculture per capita in Brunei was $32.7 in the 1970s, ranked 172nd in the world. The sector of agriculture per capita in Brunei was less than agriculture per capita in the world ($127.6) in 3.9 times, and was less than agriculture per capita in Asia ($76.7) in 2.3 times.

The growth of agriculture in Brunei was 1.4% in the 1970s, ranked 130th in the world. The growth of agriculture in Brunei (1.4%) was less than growth of agriculture in the world (2.2%), was less than growth of agriculture in Asia (2.0%).

Comparison with neighbors. The sector of agriculture in Brunei was less than in Malaysia ($2.8 billion). The value added of agriculture per capita in Brunei was less than in Malaysia ($233.8). The growth of agriculture in Brunei was less than in Malaysia (7.7%).

Comparison with leaders. The sector of agriculture in Brunei was less than in the USSR ($88.7 billion), in China ($49.5 billion), in the USA ($42.6 billion), in India ($36.0 billion), and in Japan ($25.8 billion). The value added of agriculture per capita in Brunei was less than in the USSR ($351.8), in Japan ($231.3), in the USA ($195.0), in India ($58.3), and in China ($54.2). The growth of agriculture in Brunei was greater than in Japan (0.52%), in the USA (0.34%), and in India (0.30%); but less than in the USSR (7.0%) and in China (2.4%).

The 1980s

The value added of agriculture in Brunei was $19.0 million per year in the 1980s, ranked 161st in the world, and was on a par with Liechtenstein ($19.1 million). The share in the world was 0.0021%, and 0.0055% in Asia.

The share of agriculture in the economy of Brunei was 0.44% in the 1980s, ranked 180th in the world.

The agriculture per capita in Brunei was $85.8 in the 1980s, ranked 155th in the world, and was on a par with Antigua and Barbuda ($86.0), Botswana ($85.2), Myanmar ($84.2). The value of agriculture per capita in Brunei was less than agriculture per capita in the world ($186.6) in 2.2 times, and was less than agriculture per capita in Asia ($122.8) by 30.1%.

The growth of agriculture in Brunei was 3.6% in the 1980s, ranked 51st in the world, and was on a par with Somalia (3.6%), Congo (3.7%), the USA (3.7%). The growth of agriculture in Brunei (3.6%) was greater than growth of agriculture in the world (3.1%), was less than growth of agriculture in Asia (3.8%).

Comparison with neighbors. The agriculture of Brunei was less than in Malaysia ($6.2 billion). The value added of agriculture per capita in Brunei was less than in Malaysia ($399.0). The growth of agriculture in Brunei was less than in Malaysia (3.9%).

Comparison with leaders. The Brunei's agriculture was less than in the USSR ($125.8 billion), in China ($94.9 billion), in India ($70.4 billion), in the USA ($68.7 billion), and in Japan ($49.7 billion). The value added of agriculture per capita in Brunei was less than in the USSR ($457.2), in Japan ($410.0), in the USA ($286.8), in India ($90.7), and in China ($88.5). The growth of agriculture in Brunei was greater than in the USSR (2.8%) and in Japan (0.41%); but less than in China (5.3%), in India (4.4%), and in the USA (3.7%).

The 1990s

The Brunei's agriculture was $53.0 million per year in the 1990s, ranked 175th in the world. The share in the world was 0.0047%, and 0.010% in Asia.

The share of agriculture in the economy of Brunei was 1.1% in the 1990s, ranked 194th in the world.

The sector of agriculture per capita in Brunei was $181.0 in the 1990s, ranked 113th in the world, and was on a par with the Philippines ($180.9), Algeria ($184.2), Montserrat ($184.3). The sector of agriculture per capita in Brunei was less than agriculture per capita in the world ($199.8) by 9.4%, and was greater than agriculture per capita in Asia ($151.6) by 19.4%.

The growth of agriculture in Brunei was 3.3% in the 1990s, ranked 62nd in the world, and was on a par with Norway (3.3%). The growth of agriculture in Brunei (3.3%) was greater than growth of agriculture in the world (2.2%), was greater than growth of agriculture in Asia (3.2%).

Comparison with neighbors. The value of agriculture in Brunei was less than in Malaysia ($9.4 billion). The Brunei's agriculture per capita was less than in Malaysia ($465.2). The growth of agriculture in Brunei was greater than in Malaysia (0.10%).

Comparison with leaders. The sector of agriculture in Brunei was less than in China ($139.0 billion), in the United States ($96.1 billion), in India ($91.4 billion), in Japan ($78.9 billion), and in Brazil ($36.8 billion). The agriculture per capita in Brunei was greater than in China ($112.7) and in India ($95.6); but less than in Japan ($625.5), in the USA ($363.4), and in Brazil ($228.7). The growth of agriculture in Brunei was greater than in Brazil (3.0%), in India (2.8%), in the United States (2.6%), and in Japan (-1.8%); but less than in China (4.3%).

The 2000s

The Brunei's agriculture was $85.8 million per year in the 2000s, ranked 173rd in the world, and was on a par with the Maldives ($87.4 million), Vanuatu ($87.9 million). The share in the world was 0.0055%, and 0.011% in Asia.

The share of agriculture in the economy of Brunei was 0.84% in the 2000s, ranked 191st in the world.

The value of agriculture per capita in Brunei was $238.0 in the 2000s, ranked 109th in the world, and was on a par with Eastern Europe ($238.1), Georgia ($238.1), the Marshall Islands ($237.5). The Brunei's agriculture per capita was less than agriculture per capita in the world ($240.3) by 0.97%, and was greater than agriculture per capita in Asia ($202.4) by 17.6%.

The growth of agriculture in Brunei was 3.6% in the 2000s, ranked 54th in the world, and was on a par with the USA (3.6%), Egypt (3.6%), Russia (3.6%). The growth of agriculture in Brunei (3.6%) was greater than growth of agriculture in the world (3.0%), was greater than growth of agriculture in Asia (3.1%).

Comparison with neighbors. The value of agriculture in Brunei was less than in Malaysia ($13.3 billion). The agriculture per capita in Brunei was less than in Malaysia ($523.3). The growth of agriculture in Brunei was greater than in Malaysia (3.3%).

Comparison with leaders. The Brunei's agriculture was less than in China ($297.7 billion), in India ($147.6 billion), in the United States ($122.5 billion), in Japan ($57.1 billion), and in Nigeria ($47.6 billion). The value added of agriculture per capita in Brunei was greater than in China ($224.5) and in India ($129.7); but less than in Japan ($445.6), in the USA ($416.9), and in Nigeria ($346.4). The growth of agriculture in Brunei was greater than in the USA (3.6%), in India (2.0%), and in Japan (-1.3%); but less than in Nigeria (10.1%) and in China (4.0%).

The 2010s

The value added of agriculture in Brunei was $128.5 million per year in the 2010s, ranked 173rd in the world, and was on a par with Cabo Verde ($131.7 million). The share in the world was 0.0041%, and 0.0067% in Asia.

The share of agriculture in the economy of Brunei was 0.84% in the 2010s, ranked 188th in the world.

The sector of agriculture per capita in Brunei was $312.2 in the 2010s, ranked 117th in the world, and was on a par with Jamaica ($312.5), Guinea-Bissau ($310.5), Liberia ($314.7). The Brunei's agriculture per capita was less than agriculture per capita in the world ($432.1) by 27.8%, and was less than agriculture per capita in Asia ($436.7) by 28.5%.

The growth of agriculture in Brunei was 0% in the 2010s, ranked 163rd in the world. The growth of agriculture in Brunei (0.039%) was less than growth of agriculture in the world (2.9%), was less than growth of agriculture in Asia (3.3%).

Comparison with neighbors. The Brunei's agriculture was 218.9 times lower than in Malaysia ($28.1 billion). The agriculture per capita in Brunei was 3.0 times lower than in Malaysia ($935.6). The growth of agriculture in Brunei was less than in Malaysia (2.0%).

Comparison with leaders. The sector of agriculture in Brunei was 6 894.6 times lower than in China ($886.2 billion), 2 827.3 times lower than in India ($363.4 billion), 1 402.6 times lower than in the USA ($180.3 billion), 965.1 times lower than in Indonesia ($124.1 billion), and 745.0 times lower than in Nigeria ($95.8 billion). The sector of agriculture per capita in Brunei was 11.9% higher than in India ($279.1); but 2.0 times lower than in China ($631.9), 44.7% lower than in the United States ($564.3), 41.6% lower than in Nigeria ($534.6), and 35.4% lower than in Indonesia ($483.6). The growth of agriculture in Brunei was less than in India (4.1%), in Indonesia (3.9%), in China (3.8%), in Nigeria (3.6%), and in the United States (2.0%).

Chapter V. Industry

Mining, Manufacturing, Utilities (ISIC C-E)

The sector of industry in Brunei grew from $1.3 billion per year in the 1970s to $9.6 billion per year in the 2010s, that is by $8.3 billion or 7.4 times. The change occurred at $8.4 billion due to a 7.5-fold increase in prices, as also at -$2.1 billion due to a 2.6-fold decrease in productivity, as well as at $2.1 billion due to the rise in population. The average annual growth in industry is 0.71%. The minimum value of industry was in 1970 at $206.5 million. The maximum value of industry was in 2012 at $13.4 billion.

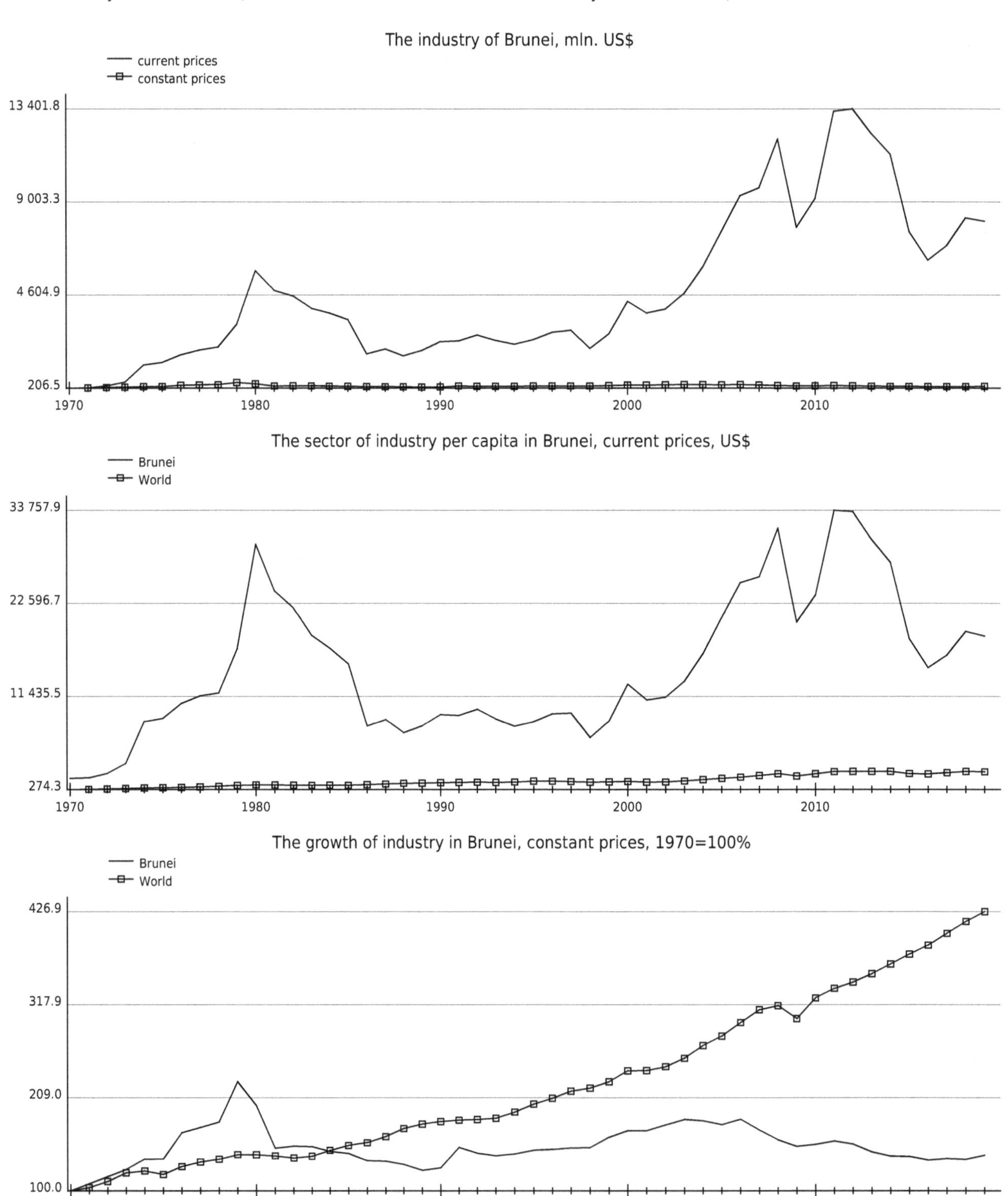

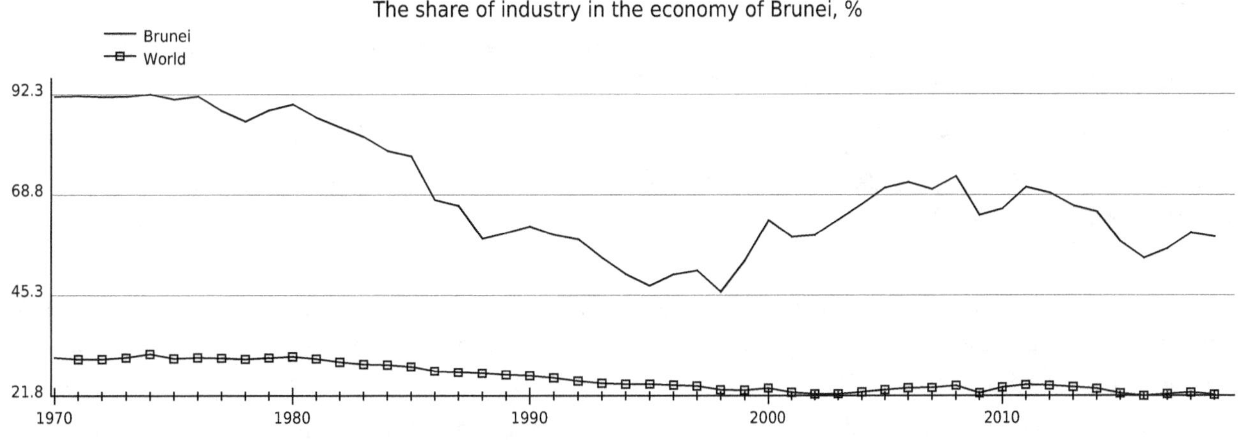

The 1970s

The industry of Brunei was $1.3 billion per year in the 1970s, ranked 68th in the world, and was on a par with Singapore ($1.3 billion). The share in the world was 0.068%, and 0.32% in Asia.

The share of industry in the economy of Brunei was 89.5% in the 1970s, ranked 1st in the world.

The value of industry per capita in Brunei was $8 281.5 in the 1970s, ranked 3rd in the world. The industry per capita in Brunei was greater than industry per capita in the world ($480.5) in 17.2 times, and was greater than industry per capita in Asia ($173.9) in 47.6 times.

The growth of industry in Brunei was 9.6% in the 1970s, ranked 18th in the world, and was on a par with Egypt (9.5%), Kenya (9.6%), the Dominican Republic (9.6%). The growth of industry in Brunei (9.6%) was greater than growth of industry in the world (4.0%), was greater than growth of industry in Asia (5.7%).

Comparison with neighbors. The Brunei's industry was less than in Malaysia ($3.2 billion). The value added of industry per capita in Brunei was greater than in Malaysia ($262.9). The growth of industry in Brunei was greater than in Malaysia (8.0%).

Comparison with leaders. The value added of industry in Brunei was less than in the USA ($450.4 billion), in the USSR ($248.8 billion), in Japan ($185.6 billion), in Germany ($158.4 billion), and in the United Kingdom ($72.6 billion). The value added of industry per capita in Brunei was greater than in the USA ($2.1 thousand), in Germany ($2.0 thousand), in Japan ($1 666.5), in the United Kingdom ($1 295.1), and in the USSR ($986.6). The growth of industry in Brunei was greater than in the USSR (5.2%), in Japan (4.5%), in the United States (2.4%), in Germany (2.1%), and in the United Kingdom (1.9%).

The 1980s

The value of industry in Brunei was $3.4 billion per year in the 1980s, ranked 65th in the world. The share in the world was 0.081%, and 0.31% in Asia.

The share of industry in the economy of Brunei was 78.1% in the 1980s, ranked 1st in the world.

The value of industry per capita in Brunei was $15 259.5 in the 1980s, ranked 1st in the world. The industry per capita in Brunei was greater than industry per capita in the world ($861.8) in 17.7 times, and was greater than industry per capita in Asia ($380.7) in 40.1 times.

The growth of industry in Brunei was -5.9% in the 1980s, ranked 181st in the world. The growth of industry in Brunei (-5.9%) was less than growth of industry in the world (2.3%), was less than growth of industry in Asia (3.5%).

Comparison with neighbors. The value of industry in Brunei was less than in Malaysia ($10.9 billion). The value added of industry per capita in Brunei was greater than in Malaysia ($701.8). The growth of industry in Brunei was less than in Malaysia (6.5%).

Comparison with leaders. The Brunei's industry was less than in the USA ($1.0 trillion), in Japan ($566.4 billion), in the USSR ($305.7 billion), in Germany ($297.5 billion), and in the UK ($171.2 billion). The value of industry per capita in Brunei was greater than in Japan ($4.7 thousand), in the United States ($4.2 thousand), in Germany ($3.8 thousand), in the United Kingdom ($3.0 thousand), and in the USSR ($1 110.8). The growth of industry in Brunei was less than in the USSR (5.3%), in Japan (4.2%), in the United States (1.9%), in the UK (1.4%), and in Germany (1.2%).

The 1990s

The Brunei's industry was $2.5 billion per year in the 1990s, ranked 83rd in the world, and was on a par with Luxembourg ($2.5 billion), Zimbabwe ($2.5 billion). The share in the world was 0.038%, and 0.11% in Asia.

The share of industry in the economy of Brunei was 52.8% in the 1990s, ranked 3rd in the world.

The industry per capita in Brunei was $8 669.7 in the 1990s, ranked 6th in the world. The sector of industry per capita in Brunei was greater than industry per capita in the world ($1 175.6) in 7.4 times, and was greater than industry per capita in Asia ($639.7) in 13.6 times.

The growth of industry in Brunei was 2.8% in the 1990s, ranked 97th in the world, and was on a par with the Americas (2.8%), Saint Kitts and Nevis (2.8%), Peru (2.8%). The growth of industry in Brunei (2.8%) was greater than growth of industry in the world (2.5%), was less than growth of industry in Asia (5.5%).

Comparison with neighbors. The industry of Brunei was less than in Malaysia ($27.4 billion). The Brunei's industry per capita was greater than in Malaysia ($1 348.3). The growth of industry in Brunei was less than in Malaysia (7.2%).

Comparison with leaders. The sector of industry in Brunei was less than in the United States ($1.5 trillion), in Japan ($1.2 trillion), in Germany ($534.0 billion), in China ($285.9 billion), and in the UK ($268.6 billion). The Brunei's industry per capita was greater than in Germany ($6.6 thousand), in the United States ($5.7 thousand), in the United Kingdom ($4.6 thousand), and in China ($231.9); but less than in Japan ($9.4 thousand). The growth of industry in Brunei was greater than in Japan (1.3%), in the UK (1.2%), and in Germany (0.33%); but less than in China (13.1%) and in the USA (2.8%).

The 2000s

The sector of industry in Brunei was $6.9 billion per year in the 2000s, ranked 78th in the world, and was on a par with the Dominican Republic ($7.0 billion), Sudan ($7.1 billion). The share in the world was 0.067%, and 0.18% in Asia.

The share of industry in the economy of Brunei was 67.4% in the 2000s, ranked 2nd in the world.

The value added of industry per capita in Brunei was $19 133.5 in the 2000s, ranked 6th in the world, and was on a par with Kuwait ($19.3 thousand). The value added of industry per capita in Brunei was greater than industry per capita in the world ($1 573.8) in 12.2 times, and was greater than industry per capita in Asia ($951.8) in 20.1 times.

The growth of industry in Brunei was -0.7% in the 2000s, ranked 187th in the world. The growth of industry in Brunei (-0.68%) was less than growth of industry in the world (2.9%), was less than growth of industry in Asia (5.7%).

Comparison with neighbors. The value of industry in Brunei was less than in Malaysia ($61.5 billion). The value of industry per capita in Brunei was greater than in Malaysia ($2.4 thousand). The growth of industry in Brunei was less than in Malaysia (2.9%).

Comparison with leaders. The value of industry in Brunei was less than in the United States ($2.1 trillion), in Japan ($1.1 trillion), in China ($1.1 trillion), in Germany ($629.4 billion), and in the United Kingdom ($345.1 billion). The value added of industry per capita in Brunei was greater than in Japan ($8.8 thousand), in Germany ($7.7 thousand), in the USA ($7.1 thousand), in the United Kingdom ($5.7 thousand), and in China ($795.3). The growth of industry in Brunei was greater than in the UK (-1.1%); but less than in China (11.1%), in the USA (1.5%), in Germany (0.19%), and in Japan (0.15%).

The 2010s

The industry of Brunei was $9.6 billion per year in the 2010s, ranked 86th in the world, and was on a par with Trinidad and Tobago ($9.7 billion), Equatorial Guinea ($9.7 billion), Croatia ($9.7 billion). The share in the world was 0.057%, and 0.12% in Asia.

The share of industry in the economy of Brunei was 63.3% in the 2010s, ranked 2nd in the world.

The Brunei's industry per capita was $23 432.4 in the 2010s, ranked 5th in the world, and was on a par with Kuwait ($23.8 thousand), Norway ($24.0 thousand). The value of industry per capita in Brunei was greater than industry per capita in the world ($2 320.9) in 10.1 times, and was greater than industry per capita in Asia ($1 847.0) in 12.7 times.

The growth of industry in Brunei was -0.7% in the 2010s, ranked 184th in the world. The growth of industry in Brunei (-0.70%) was less than growth of industry in the world (3.5%), was less than growth of industry in Asia (5.6%).

Comparison with neighbors. The Brunei's industry was 11.4 times lower than in Malaysia ($109.8 billion). The value added of industry per capita in Brunei was 6.4 times higher than in Malaysia ($3.7 thousand). The growth of industry in Brunei was less than in Malaysia (4.1%).

Comparison with leaders. The industry of Brunei was 381.8 times lower than in China ($3.7 trillion), 284.2 times lower than in the USA ($2.7 trillion), 123.4 times lower than in Japan ($1.2 trillion), 87.1 times lower than in Germany ($840.0 billion), and 46.0 times lower than in India ($443.4 billion). The value added of industry per capita in Brunei was 2.3 times higher than in Germany ($10.3 thousand), 2.5 times higher than in Japan ($9.3 thousand), 2.7 times higher than in the USA ($8.6 thousand), 8.9 times higher than in China ($2.6 thousand), and 68.8 times higher than in India ($340.6). The growth of industry in Brunei was less than in China (7.5%), in India (6.5%), in Germany (3.2%), in Japan (2.6%), and in the United States (2.2%).

Chapter 5.1. Manufacturing

(ISIC D)

The manufacturing of Brunei rose from $272.3 million per year in the 1970s to $2.2 billion per year in the 2010s, that is by $2.0 billion or 8.2 times. The change occurred at $1.8 billion due to a 5.5-fold increase in prices, as also at -$300.2 million due to a 1.7-fold decrease in productivity, as well as at $435.4 million due to the expansion in population. The average annual growth in manufacturing is 2.6%. The minimum value of manufacturing was in 1970 at $38.7 million. The maximum value of manufacturing was in 2012 at $3.2 billion.

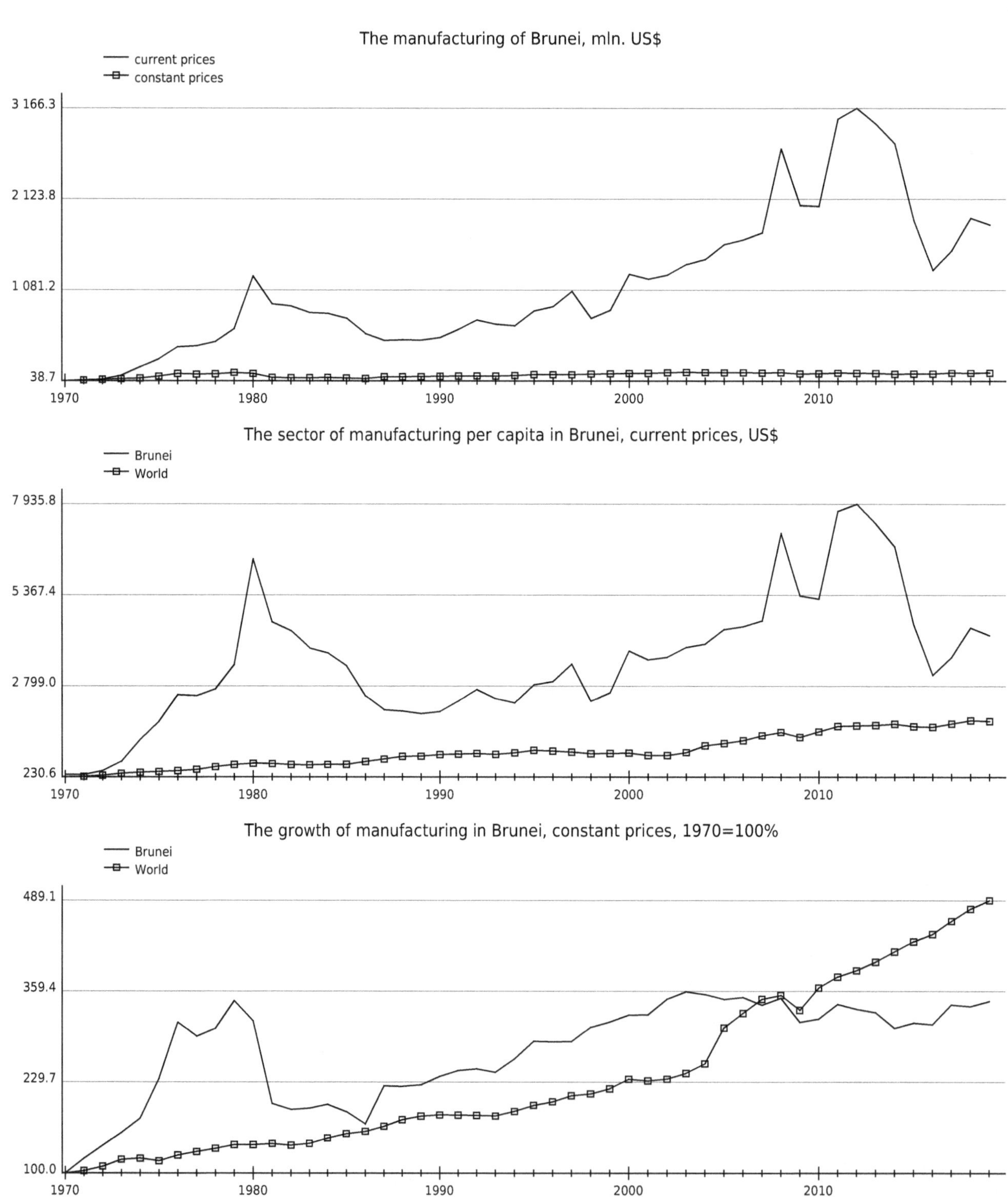

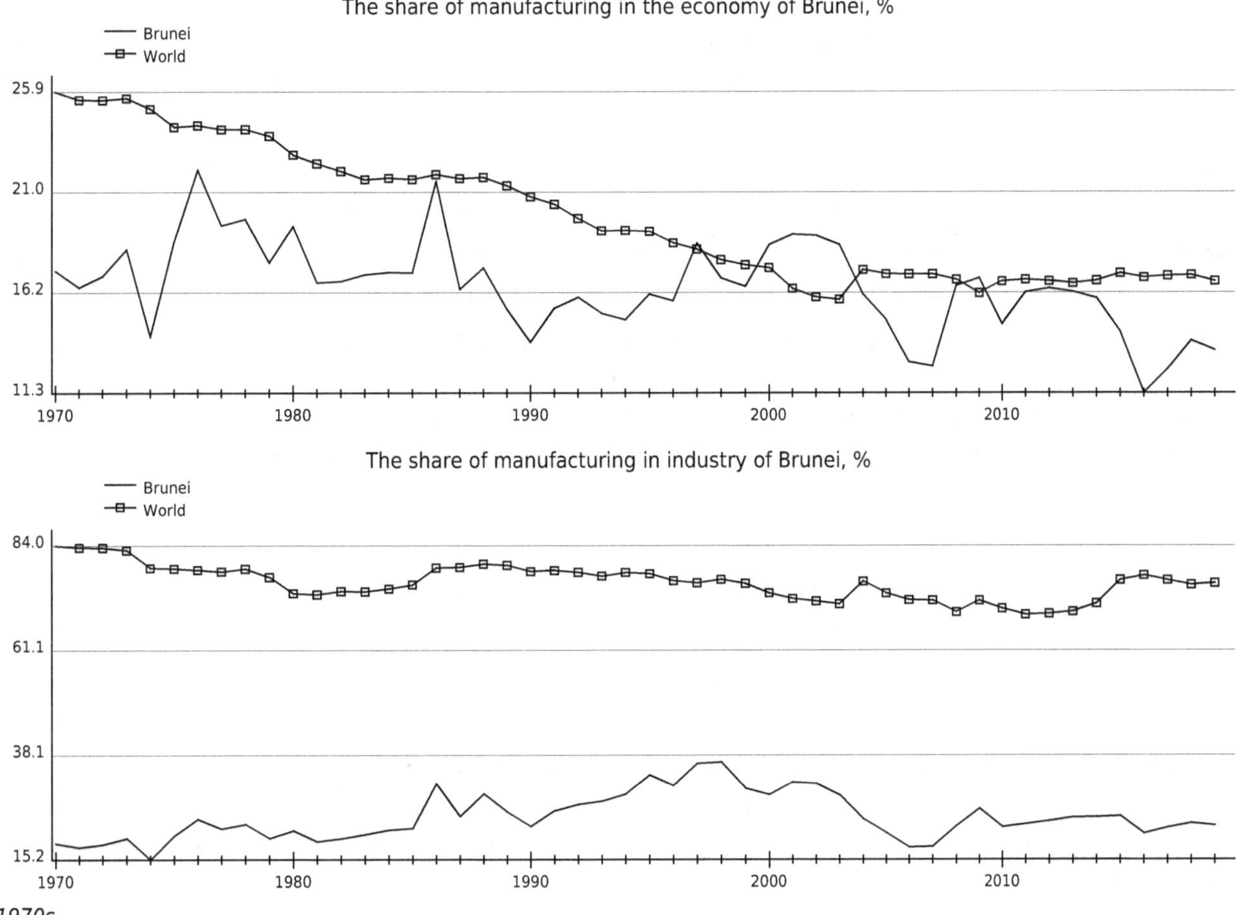

The share of manufacturing in the economy of Brunei, %

The share of manufacturing in industry of Brunei, %

The 1970s

The manufacturing of Brunei was $272.3 million per year in the 1970s, ranked 93rd in the world, and was on a par with Bolivia ($267.5 million), Sudan ($266.0 million). The share in the world was 0.018%, and 0.11% in Asia.

The share of manufacturing in the economy of Brunei was 18.6% in the 1970s, ranked 67th in the world, and was on a par with Iceland (18.7%).

The value of manufacturing per capita in Brunei was $1 718.9 in the 1970s, ranked 8th in the world, and was on a par with the USA ($1 731.8), Northern America ($1 698.2), Germany ($1 752.1). The value added of manufacturing per capita in Brunei was greater than manufacturing per capita in the world ($383.2) in 4.5 times, and was greater than manufacturing per capita in Asia ($104.9) in 16.4 times.

The growth of manufacturing in Brunei was 14.8% in the 1970s, ranked 5th in the world. The growth of manufacturing in Brunei (14.8%) was greater than growth of manufacturing in the world (3.8%), was greater than growth of manufacturing in Asia (5.6%).

Comparison with neighbors. The sector of manufacturing in Brunei was less than in Malaysia ($1.9 billion). The manufacturing per capita in Brunei was greater than in Malaysia ($158.1). The growth of manufacturing in Brunei was greater than in Malaysia (12.7%).

Comparison with leaders. The Brunei's manufacturing was less than in the United States ($378.0 billion), in the USSR ($248.8 billion), in Japan ($169.3 billion), in Germany ($138.0 billion), and in France ($64.5 billion). The sector of manufacturing per capita in Brunei was greater than in Japan ($1 520.6), in France ($1 203.0), and in the USSR ($986.6); but less than in Germany ($1 752.1) and in the United States ($1 731.8). The growth of manufacturing in Brunei was greater than in the USSR (5.2%), in Japan (4.5%), in France (3.5%), in the USA (2.7%), and in Germany (2.1%).

The 1980s

The manufacturing of Brunei was $755.5 million per year in the 1980s, ranked 84th in the world, and was on a par with Panama ($769.2 million). The share in the world was 0.024%, and 0.10% in Asia.

The share of manufacturing in the economy of Brunei was 17.4% in the 1980s, ranked 69th in the world, and was on a par with Jordan

(17.4%), Australasia (17.3%), Kenya (17.3%).

The sector of manufacturing per capita in Brunei was $3 404.8 in the 1980s, ranked 6th in the world, and was on a par with Luxembourg ($3.4 thousand). The manufacturing per capita in Brunei was greater than manufacturing per capita in the world ($661.2) in 5.1 times, and was greater than manufacturing per capita in Asia ($256.6) in 13.3 times.

The growth of manufacturing in Brunei was -4.2% in the 1980s, ranked 180th in the world. The growth of manufacturing in Brunei (-4.2%) was less than growth of manufacturing in the world (2.6%), was less than growth of manufacturing in Asia (5.4%).

Comparison with neighbors. The value added of manufacturing in Brunei was less than in Malaysia ($6.3 billion). The manufacturing per capita in Brunei was greater than in Malaysia ($408.0). The growth of manufacturing in Brunei was less than in Malaysia (8.7%).

Comparison with leaders. The Brunei's manufacturing was less than in the United States ($789.4 billion), in Japan ($501.0 billion), in the USSR ($305.7 billion), in Germany ($258.7 billion), and in Italy ($134.1 billion). The sector of manufacturing per capita in Brunei was greater than in Germany ($3.3 thousand), in the USA ($3.3 thousand), in Italy ($2.4 thousand), and in the USSR ($1 110.8); but less than in Japan ($4.1 thousand). The growth of manufacturing in Brunei was less than in the USSR (5.3%), in Japan (4.4%), in Italy (2.5%), in the USA (1.9%), and in Germany (1.2%).

The 1990s

The value added of manufacturing in Brunei was $768.2 million per year in the 1990s, ranked 103rd in the world, and was on a par with DR Congo ($774.3 million), Bahrain ($781.3 million), Mauritius ($750.3 million). The share in the world was 0.015%, and 0.049% in Asia.

The share of manufacturing in the economy of Brunei was 16.0% in the 1990s, ranked 87th in the world, and was on a par with Cameroon (15.9%).

The value added of manufacturing per capita in Brunei was $2 622.6 in the 1990s, ranked 25th in the world, and was on a par with Australia ($2.6 thousand), Australasia ($2.6 thousand), Southern Europe ($2.6 thousand). The Brunei's manufacturing per capita was greater than manufacturing per capita in the world ($908.4) in 2.9 times, and was greater than manufacturing per capita in Asia ($456.2) in 5.7 times.

The growth of manufacturing in Brunei was 3.4% in the 1990s, ranked 78th in the world. The growth of manufacturing in Brunei (3.4%) was greater than growth of manufacturing in the world (2.0%), was less than growth of manufacturing in Asia (3.5%).

Comparison with neighbors. The value of manufacturing in Brunei was less than in Malaysia ($20.1 billion). The value added of manufacturing per capita in Brunei was greater than in Malaysia ($990.2). The growth of manufacturing in Brunei was less than in Malaysia (9.7%).

Comparison with leaders. The value added of manufacturing in Brunei was less than in the United States ($1.2 trillion), in Japan ($1.0 trillion), in Germany ($468.8 billion), in Italy ($227.8 billion), and in France ($215.0 billion). The Brunei's manufacturing per capita was less than in Japan ($8.3 thousand), in Germany ($5.8 thousand), in the United States ($4.7 thousand), in Italy ($4.0 thousand), and in France ($3.6 thousand). The growth of manufacturing in Brunei was greater than in the USA (3.2%), in France (2.4%), in Italy (1.2%), in Japan (1.1%), and in Germany (0.26%).

The 2000s

The value added of manufacturing in Brunei was $1.6 billion per year in the 2000s, ranked 101st in the world. The share in the world was 0.022%, and 0.063% in Asia.

The share of manufacturing in the economy of Brunei was 15.9% in the 2000s, ranked 70th in the world, and was on a par with Cameroon (15.9%), Ecuador (16.0%), Southern Europe (16.0%).

The manufacturing per capita in Brunei was $4 515.9 in the 2000s, ranked 22nd in the world, and was on a par with Canada ($4.5 thousand). The manufacturing per capita in Brunei was greater than manufacturing per capita in the world ($1 138.1) in 4.0 times, and was greater than manufacturing per capita in Asia ($659.1) in 6.9 times.

The growth of manufacturing in Brunei was -0% in the 2000s, ranked 164th in the world. The growth of manufacturing in Brunei (-0.015%) was less than growth of manufacturing in the world (4.2%), was less than growth of manufacturing in Asia (10.5%).

Comparison with neighbors. The value of manufacturing in Brunei was less than in Malaysia ($39.6 billion). The value added of manufacturing per capita in Brunei was greater than in Malaysia ($1 556.7). The growth of manufacturing in Brunei was less than in

Malaysia (4.2%).

Comparison with leaders. The value added of manufacturing in Brunei was less than in the United States ($1.6 trillion), in China ($1.1 trillion), in Japan ($992.9 billion), in Germany ($551.4 billion), and in Italy ($277.2 billion). The value of manufacturing per capita in Brunei was greater than in China ($815.3); but less than in Japan ($7.7 thousand), in Germany ($6.8 thousand), in the United States ($5.6 thousand), and in Italy ($4.8 thousand). The growth of manufacturing in Brunei was greater than in Italy (-1.3%); but less than in the USA (1.6%), in Japan (0.32%), and in Germany (0.097%).

The 2010s

The value added of manufacturing in Brunei was $2.2 billion per year in the 2010s, ranked 110th in the world. The share in the world was 0.018%, and 0.036% in Asia.

The share of manufacturing in the economy of Brunei was 14.7% in the 2010s, ranked 68th in the world, and was on a par with Ecuador (14.7%), Cuba (14.6%).

The Brunei's manufacturing per capita was $5 454.9 in the 2010s, ranked 20th in the world, and was on a par with the Netherlands ($5.4 thousand), Luxembourg ($5.4 thousand). The value of manufacturing per capita in Brunei was greater than manufacturing per capita in the world ($1 697.4) in 3.2 times, and was greater than manufacturing per capita in Asia ($1 401.2) in 3.9 times.

The growth of manufacturing in Brunei was 0.9% in the 2010s, ranked 161st in the world. The growth of manufacturing in Brunei (0.92%) was less than growth of manufacturing in the world (3.9%), was less than growth of manufacturing in Asia (6.0%).

Comparison with neighbors. The value added of manufacturing in Brunei was 31.7 times lower than in Malaysia ($71.1 billion). The Brunei's manufacturing per capita was 2.3 times higher than in Malaysia ($2.4 thousand). The growth of manufacturing in Brunei was less than in Malaysia (5.5%).

Comparison with leaders. The manufacturing of Brunei was 1 387.1 times lower than in China ($3.1 trillion), 922.0 times lower than in the USA ($2.1 trillion), 472.0 times lower than in Japan ($1.1 trillion), 327.4 times lower than in Germany ($735.2 billion), and 173.9 times lower than in South Korea ($390.5 billion). The sector of manufacturing per capita in Brunei was 2.5 times higher than in China ($2.2 thousand); but 39.3% lower than in Germany ($9.0 thousand), 34.2% lower than in Japan ($8.3 thousand), 29.4% lower than in Republic of Korea ($7.7 thousand), and 15.8% lower than in the USA ($6.5 thousand). The growth of manufacturing in Brunei was less than in China (7.5%), in South Korea (3.8%), in Germany (3.5%), in Japan (3.0%), and in the United States (1.9%).

Chapter VI. Construction

(ISIC F)

The value of construction in Brunei increased from $10.0 million per year in the 1970s to $340.8 million per year in the 2010s, that is by $330.8 million or 34.2 times. The change occurred at $306.1 million due to a 9.8-fold increase in prices, as also at $8.8 million due to a 1.3-fold increase in productivity, as well as at $15.9 million due to the growing in population. The average annual growth in construction is 4.4%. The minimum value of construction was in 1970 at $1.3 million. The maximum value of construction was in 2013 at $444.2 million.

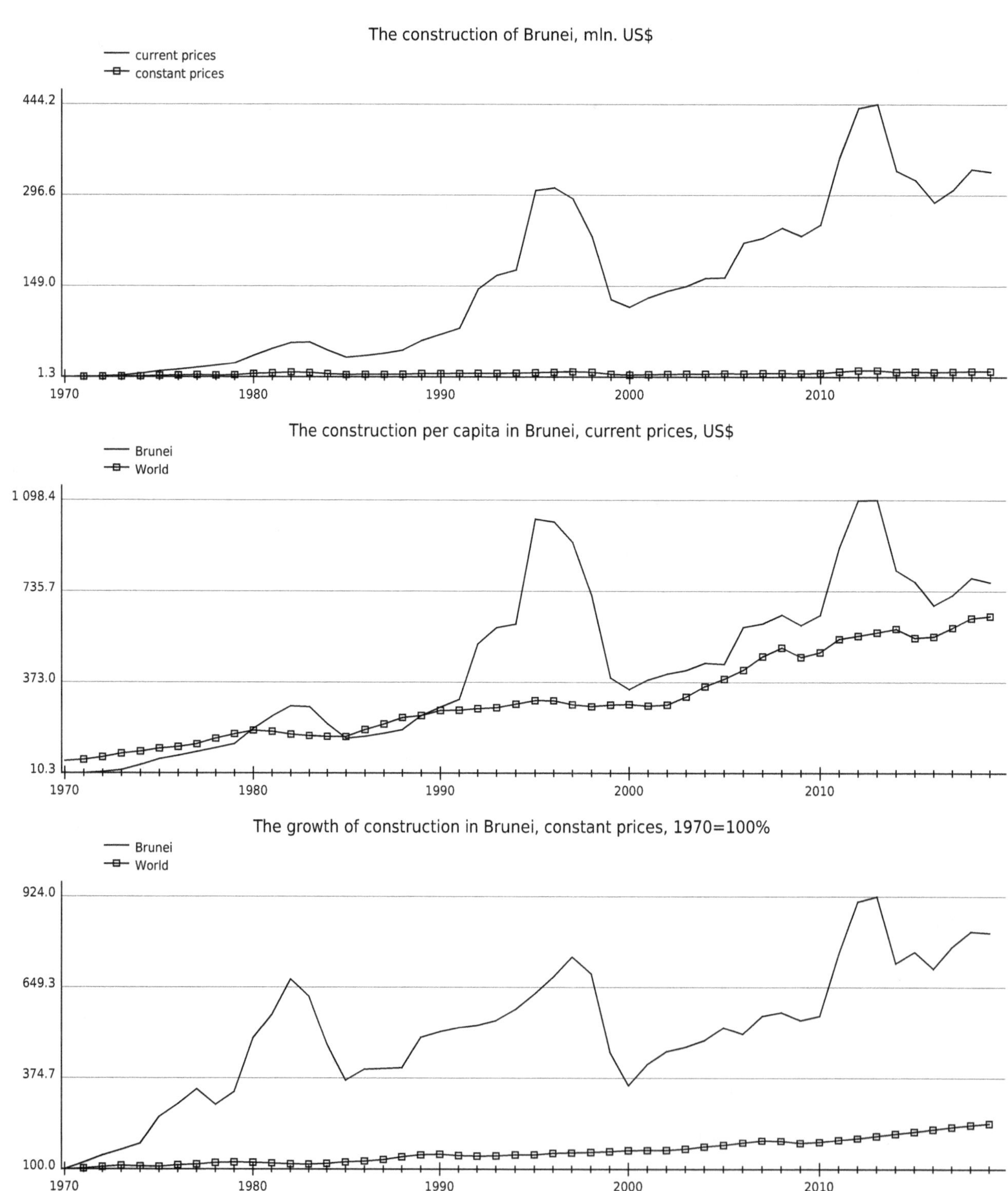

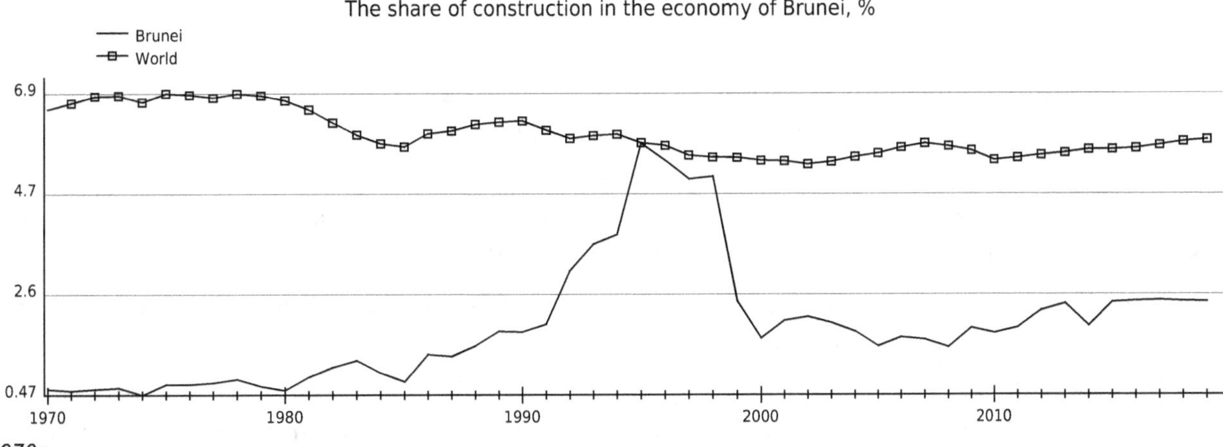

The 1970s

The sector of construction in Brunei was $10.0 million per year in the 1970s, ranked 153rd in the world, and was on a par with Laos ($10.1 million). The share in the world was 0.0023%, and 0.012% in Asia.

The share of construction in the economy of Brunei was 0.68% in the 1970s, ranked 185th in the world.

The value of construction per capita in Brunei was $62.9 in the 1970s, ranked 83rd in the world, and was on a par with South Africa ($62.9), Micronesia ($63.3). The value added of construction per capita in Brunei was less than construction per capita in the world ($106.1) by 40.7%, and was greater than construction per capita in Asia ($34.4) by 82.8%.

The growth of construction in Brunei was 14.3% in the 1970s, ranked 13th in the world, and was on a par with Guatemala (14.3%), Trinidad and Tobago (14.3%), Bahrain (14.4%). The growth of construction in Brunei (14.3%) was greater than growth of construction in the world (2.1%), was greater than growth of construction in Asia (5.1%).

Comparison with neighbors. The sector of construction in Brunei was less than in Malaysia ($431.5 million). The construction per capita in Brunei was greater than in Malaysia ($35.8). The growth of construction in Brunei was greater than in Malaysia (11.2%).

Comparison with leaders. The construction of Brunei was less than in the United States ($81.1 billion), in the USSR ($52.5 billion), in Japan ($43.5 billion), in Germany ($33.8 billion), and in France ($22.4 billion). The value of construction per capita in Brunei was less than in Germany ($428.6), in France ($417.3), in Japan ($390.8), in the United States ($371.5), and in the USSR ($208.1). The growth of construction in Brunei was greater than in the USSR (6.5%), in Japan (3.4%), in France (2.0%), in Germany (0.66%), and in the USA (0.31%).

The 1980s

The construction of Brunei was $45.8 million per year in the 1980s, ranked 139th in the world, and was on a par with Benin ($44.8 million). The share in the world was 0.0051%, and 0.019% in Asia.

The share of construction in the economy of Brunei was 1.1% in the 1980s, ranked 183rd in the world.

The sector of construction per capita in Brunei was $206.4 in the 1980s, ranked 65th in the world, and was on a par with Portugal ($210.8). The Brunei's construction per capita was greater than construction per capita in the world ($186.2) by 10.9%, and was greater than construction per capita in Asia ($83.3) in 2.5 times.

The growth of construction in Brunei was 4.1% in the 1980s, ranked 56th in the world, and was on a par with Mali (4.1%). The growth of construction in Brunei (4.1%) was greater than growth of construction in the world (1.7%), was greater than growth of construction in Asia (2.7%).

Comparison with neighbors. The value added of construction in Brunei was less than in Malaysia ($1.2 billion). The construction per capita in Brunei was greater than in Malaysia ($77.0). The growth of construction in Brunei was greater than in Malaysia (3.1%).

Comparison with leaders. The value of construction in Brunei was less than in the United States ($180.6 billion), in Japan ($138.7 billion), in the USSR ($72.1 billion), in Germany ($57.8 billion), and in France ($42.5 billion). The Brunei's construction per capita was less than in Japan ($1 143.9), in the United States ($754.4), in France ($751.9), in Germany ($740.2), and in the USSR ($262.0). The growth of construction in Brunei was greater than in Japan (2.1%), in the USA (1.1%), in France (0.67%), and in Germany (-0.52%);

but less than in the USSR (6.2%).

The 1990s

The value of construction in Brunei was $189.6 million per year in the 1990s, ranked 127th in the world, and was on a par with Macedonia ($187.7 million), Polynesia ($186.9 million), Monaco ($186.5 million). The share in the world was 0.012%, and 0.034% in Asia.

The share of construction in the economy of Brunei was 3.9% in the 1990s, ranked 162nd in the world, and was on a par with the United States (4.0%), the Federated States of Micronesia (3.9%), Melanesia (4.0%).

The value added of construction per capita in Brunei was $647.4 in the 1990s, ranked 46th in the world. The value added of construction per capita in Brunei was greater than construction per capita in the world ($278.6) in 2.3 times, and was greater than construction per capita in Asia ($158.8) in 4.1 times.

The growth of construction in Brunei was -0.9% in the 1990s, ranked 156th in the world. The growth of construction in Brunei (-0.92%) was less than growth of construction in the world (0.71%), was less than growth of construction in Asia (2.3%).

Comparison with neighbors. The construction of Brunei was less than in Malaysia ($4.1 billion). The construction per capita in Brunei was greater than in Malaysia ($199.7). The growth of construction in Brunei was less than in Malaysia (8.2%).

Comparison with leaders. The sector of construction in Brunei was less than in Japan ($343.2 billion), in the USA ($299.1 billion), in Germany ($125.2 billion), in the United Kingdom ($69.8 billion), and in France ($68.8 billion). The value of construction per capita in Brunei was less than in Japan ($2.7 thousand), in Germany ($1 552.3), in the UK ($1 205.1), in France ($1 158.8), and in the USA ($1 131.2). The growth of construction in Brunei was greater than in Japan (-1.0%); but less than in the United States (1.8%), in Germany (-0.047%), in the UK (-0.34%), and in France (-0.65%).

The 2000s

The Brunei's construction was $178.0 million per year in the 2000s, ranked 150th in the world, and was on a par with Tajikistan ($182.4 million). The share in the world was 0.0072%, and 0.025% in Asia.

The share of construction in the economy of Brunei was 1.7% in the 2000s, ranked 208th in the world.

The sector of construction per capita in Brunei was $493.5 in the 2000s, ranked 74th in the world, and was on a par with Central America ($493.5), Libya ($494.5), Polynesia ($497.9). The sector of construction per capita in Brunei was greater than construction per capita in the world ($381.3) by 29.4%, and was greater than construction per capita in Asia ($181.9) in 2.7 times.

The growth of construction in Brunei was 1.9% in the 2000s, ranked 148th in the world. The growth of construction in Brunei (1.9%) was greater than growth of construction in the world (1.5%), was less than growth of construction in Asia (4.4%).

Comparison with neighbors. The value added of construction in Brunei was less than in Malaysia ($4.6 billion). The value added of construction per capita in Brunei was greater than in Malaysia ($182.5). The growth of construction in Brunei was less than in Malaysia (2.4%).

Comparison with leaders. The value added of construction in Brunei was less than in the USA ($583.0 billion), in Japan ($270.5 billion), in China ($150.1 billion), in the United Kingdom ($132.1 billion), and in Spain ($111.8 billion). The Brunei's construction per capita was greater than in China ($113.1); but less than in Spain ($2.6 thousand), in the United Kingdom ($2.2 thousand), in Japan ($2.1 thousand), and in the USA ($1 983.7). The growth of construction in Brunei was greater than in Spain (1.7%), in the United Kingdom (0.17%), in the United States (-2.6%), and in Japan (-3.9%); but less than in China (11.9%).

The 2010s

The value of construction in Brunei was $340.8 million per year in the 2010s, ranked 152nd in the world, and was on a par with Niger ($338.7 million), Guyana ($346.1 million). The share in the world was 0.0081%, and 0.020% in Asia.

The share of construction in the economy of Brunei was 2.2% in the 2010s, ranked 200th in the world.

The sector of construction per capita in Brunei was $827.8 in the 2010s, ranked 65th in the world, and was on a par with Venezuela ($825.1), Turkey ($818.9). The value of construction per capita in Brunei was greater than construction per capita in the world ($572.1) by 44.7%, and was greater than construction per capita in Asia ($392.9) in 2.1 times.

The growth of construction in Brunei was 4% in the 2010s, ranked 87th in the world. The growth of construction in Brunei (4.0%) was greater than growth of construction in the world (2.9%), was less than growth of construction in Asia (5.6%).

Comparison with neighbors. The value added of construction in Brunei was 40.6 times lower than in Malaysia ($13.8 billion). The value of construction per capita in Brunei was 79.9% higher than in Malaysia ($460.1). The growth of construction in Brunei was less than in Malaysia (8.2%).

Comparison with leaders. The construction of Brunei was 2 145.1 times lower than in China ($731.1 billion), 1 997.5 times lower than in the USA ($680.8 billion), 817.6 times lower than in Japan ($278.7 billion), 493.2 times lower than in India ($168.1 billion), and 449.6 times lower than in Germany ($153.2 billion). The value of construction per capita in Brunei was 58.8% higher than in China ($521.3) and 6.4 times higher than in India ($129.1); but 2.6 times lower than in Japan ($2.2 thousand), 2.6 times lower than in the United States ($2.1 thousand), and 2.3 times lower than in Germany ($1 871.9). The growth of construction in Brunei was greater than in Germany (1.8%), in Japan (1.7%), and in the USA (1.4%); but less than in China (8.2%) and in India (5.2%).

Chapter VII. Transportation

Transport, storage and communication (ISIC I)

The sector of transportation in Brunei increased from $9.3 million per year in the 1970s to $504.2 million per year in the 2010s, that is by $494.9 million or 54.2 times. The change occurred at $365.0 million due to a 3.6-fold increase in prices, as also at $115.1 million due to a 5.8-fold increase in productivity, as well as at $14.9 million due to the growth in population. The average annual growth in transportation is 8.6%. The minimum value of transportation was in 1970 at $1.1 million. The maximum value of transportation was in 2013 at $603.0 million.

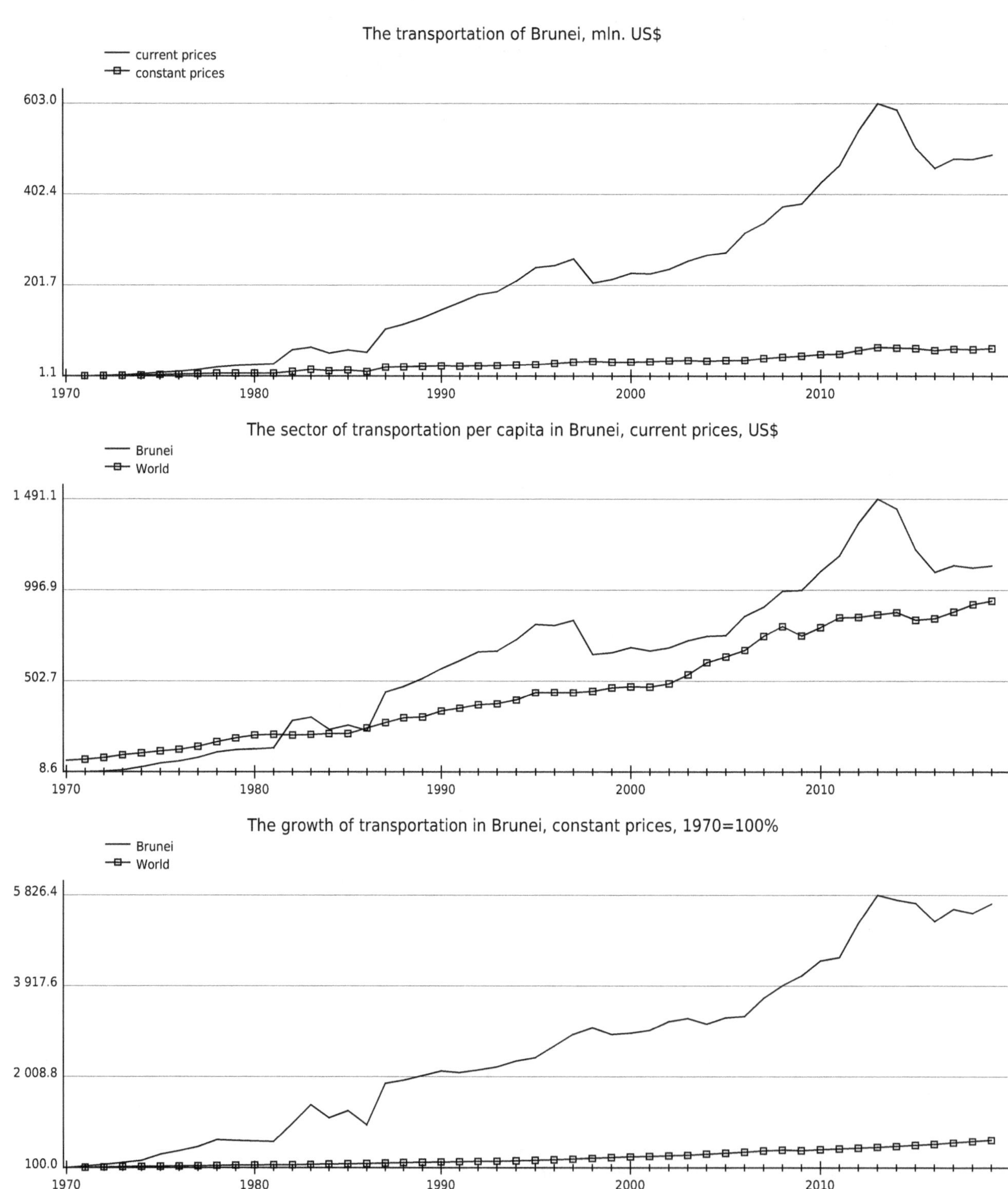

The transportation of Brunei, mln. US$

The sector of transportation per capita in Brunei, current prices, US$

The growth of transportation in Brunei, constant prices, 1970=100%

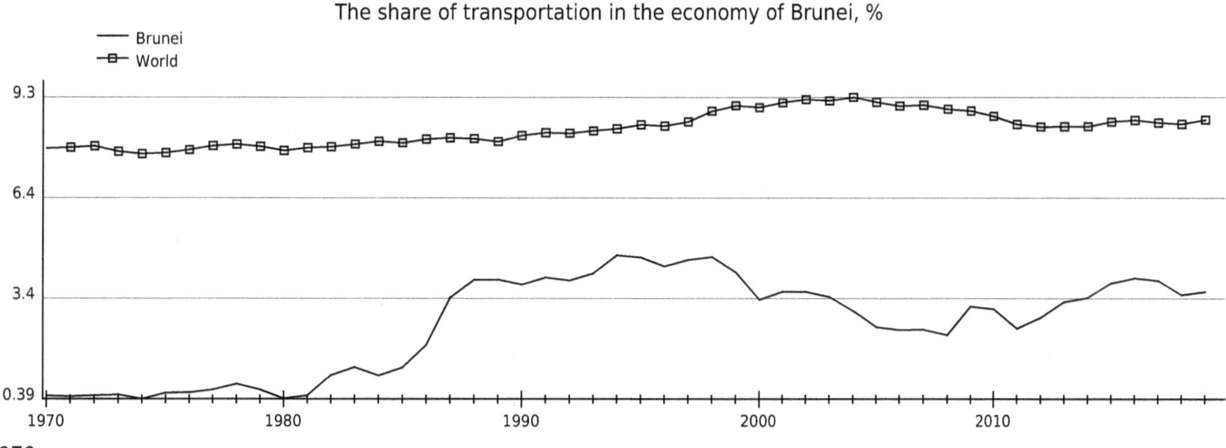

The 1970s

The value added of transportation in Brunei was $9.3 million per year in the 1970s, ranked 149th in the world. The share in the world was 0.0019%, and 0.012% in Asia.

The share of transportation in the economy of Brunei was 0.63% in the 1970s, ranked 182nd in the world.

The value of transportation per capita in Brunei was $58.7 in the 1970s, ranked 89th in the world, and was on a par with Saint Kitts and Nevis ($58.3), Montserrat ($59.4). The value of transportation per capita in Brunei was less than transportation per capita in the world ($122.3) in 2.1 times, and was greater than transportation per capita in Asia ($34.3) by 71.0%.

The growth of transportation in Brunei was 23.5% in the 1970s, ranked 1st in the world. The growth of transportation in Brunei (23.5%) was greater than growth of transportation in the world (4.6%), was greater than growth of transportation in Asia (4.1%).

Comparison with neighbors. The value added of transportation in Brunei was less than in Malaysia ($486.5 million). The transportation per capita in Brunei was greater than in Malaysia ($40.3). The growth of transportation in Brunei was greater than in Malaysia (12.6%).

Comparison with leaders. The value added of transportation in Brunei was less than in the USA ($168.6 billion), in Japan ($46.4 billion), in Germany ($29.6 billion), in the USSR ($28.8 billion), and in France ($24.0 billion). The value of transportation per capita in Brunei was less than in the United States ($772.4), in France ($447.4), in Japan ($416.6), in Germany ($376.1), and in the USSR ($114.0). The growth of transportation in Brunei was greater than in the USSR (8.1%), in the USA (4.2%), in France (4.1%), in Germany (3.0%), and in Japan (1.7%).

The 1980s

The value added of transportation in Brunei was $69.3 million per year in the 1980s, ranked 128th in the world, and was on a par with Suriname ($69.1 million), Togo ($68.9 million), Burkina Faso ($68.0 million). The share in the world was 0.0059%, and 0.028% in Asia.

The share of transportation in the economy of Brunei was 1.6% in the 1980s, ranked 181st in the world, and was on a par with Gambia (1.6%).

The Brunei's transportation per capita was $312.1 in the 1980s, ranked 54th in the world, and was on a par with Montserrat ($319.8). The sector of transportation per capita in Brunei was greater than transportation per capita in the world ($242.0) by 28.9%, and was greater than transportation per capita in Asia ($86.8) in 3.6 times.

The growth of transportation in Brunei was 11.8% in the 1980s, ranked 3rd in the world. The growth of transportation in Brunei (11.8%) was greater than growth of transportation in the world (3.4%), was greater than growth of transportation in Asia (5.2%).

Comparison with neighbors. The sector of transportation in Brunei was less than in Malaysia ($1.8 billion). The transportation per capita in Brunei was greater than in Malaysia ($115.9). The growth of transportation in Brunei was greater than in Malaysia (8.7%).

Comparison with leaders. The sector of transportation in Brunei was less than in the United States ($394.9 billion), in Japan ($147.7 billion), in Germany ($56.6 billion), in France ($56.2 billion), and in the United Kingdom ($53.0 billion). The value added of transportation per capita in Brunei was less than in the USA ($1 649.2), in Japan ($1 217.8), in France ($993.7), in the United Kingdom ($938.7), and in Germany ($725.5). The growth of transportation in Brunei was greater than in France (5.4%), in Japan

(4.7%), in the United States (3.6%), in the UK (3.0%), and in Germany (1.8%).

The 1990s

The Brunei's transportation was $205.6 million per year in the 1990s, ranked 129th in the world, and was on a par with Turkmenistan ($204.1 million), Namibia ($208.7 million), New Caledonia ($202.2 million). The share in the world was 0.0088%, and 0.033% in Asia.

The share of transportation in the economy of Brunei was 4.3% in the 1990s, ranked 184th in the world.

The transportation per capita in Brunei was $702.1 in the 1990s, ranked 48th in the world, and was on a par with South Korea ($702.9), Portugal ($694.3), Montserrat ($688.9). The transportation per capita in Brunei was greater than transportation per capita in the world ($409.5) by 71.4%, and was greater than transportation per capita in Asia ($177.2) in 4.0 times.

The growth of transportation in Brunei was 3.6% in the 1990s, ranked 125th in the world, and was on a par with Nicaragua (3.6%), Colombia (3.6%), Samoa (3.6%). The growth of transportation in Brunei (3.6%) was less than growth of transportation in the world (4.0%), was less than growth of transportation in Asia (5.4%).

Comparison with neighbors. The value of transportation in Brunei was less than in Malaysia ($4.8 billion). The sector of transportation per capita in Brunei was greater than in Malaysia ($236.7). The growth of transportation in Brunei was less than in Malaysia (9.2%).

Comparison with leaders. The value of transportation in Brunei was less than in the United States ($702.6 billion), in Japan ($373.9 billion), in Germany ($144.3 billion), in France ($118.7 billion), and in the UK ($117.6 billion). The value of transportation per capita in Brunei was less than in Japan ($3.0 thousand), in the United States ($2.7 thousand), in the UK ($2.0 thousand), in France ($1 999.2), and in Germany ($1 789.0). The growth of transportation in Brunei was greater than in Japan (3.0%); but less than in the USA (5.0%), in France (4.8%), in the United Kingdom (4.7%), and in Germany (3.9%).

The 2000s

The value added of transportation in Brunei was $290.3 million per year in the 2000s, ranked 146th in the world, and was on a par with Papua New Guinea ($292.6 million). The share in the world was 0.0072%, and 0.028% in Asia.

The share of transportation in the economy of Brunei was 2.8% in the 2000s, ranked 208th in the world.

The transportation per capita in Brunei was $804.8 in the 2000s, ranked 68th in the world, and was on a par with Palau ($818.6), Grenada ($822.1). The sector of transportation per capita in Brunei was greater than transportation per capita in the world ($621.1) by 29.6%, and was greater than transportation per capita in Asia ($264.8) in 3.0 times.

The growth of transportation in Brunei was 3.6% in the 2000s, ranked 137th in the world, and was on a par with Montenegro (3.6%). The growth of transportation in Brunei (3.6%) was less than growth of transportation in the world (3.9%), was less than growth of transportation in Asia (5.4%).

Comparison with neighbors. The value of transportation in Brunei was less than in Malaysia ($9.8 billion). The value added of transportation per capita in Brunei was greater than in Malaysia ($383.9). The growth of transportation in Brunei was less than in Malaysia (6.1%).

Comparison with leaders. The Brunei's transportation was less than in the United States ($1.2 trillion), in Japan ($468.5 billion), in Germany ($228.2 billion), in the United Kingdom ($215.9 billion), and in France ($185.6 billion). The Brunei's transportation per capita was less than in the USA ($4.0 thousand), in Japan ($3.7 thousand), in the United Kingdom ($3.6 thousand), in France ($3.0 thousand), and in Germany ($2.8 thousand). The growth of transportation in Brunei was greater than in Germany (3.4%), in the UK (3.1%), in the United States (3.1%), in France (2.7%), and in Japan (1.5%).

The 2010s

The sector of transportation in Brunei was $504.2 million per year in the 2010s, ranked 152nd in the world, and was on a par with Fiji ($492.2 million). The share in the world was 0.0079%, and 0.027% in Asia.

The share of transportation in the economy of Brunei was 3.3% in the 2010s, ranked 208th in the world.

The transportation per capita in Brunei was $1 224.7 in the 2010s, ranked 68th in the world, and was on a par with Saudi Arabia ($1 247.0). The transportation per capita in Brunei was greater than transportation per capita in the world ($864.8) by 41.6%, and was greater than transportation per capita in Asia ($430.2) in 2.8 times.

The growth of transportation in Brunei was 3.2% in the 2010s, ranked 134th in the world, and was on a par with Tunisia (3.2%), French Polynesia (3.2%). The growth of transportation in Brunei (3.2%) was less than growth of transportation in the world (4.0%), was less than growth of transportation in Asia (4.7%).

Comparison with neighbors. The Brunei's transportation was 55.0 times lower than in Malaysia ($27.7 billion). The sector of transportation per capita in Brunei was 32.9% higher than in Malaysia ($921.2). The growth of transportation in Brunei was less than in Malaysia (7.5%).

Comparison with leaders. The sector of transportation in Brunei was 3 547.0 times lower than in the United States ($1.8 trillion), 1 050.8 times lower than in Japan ($529.8 billion), 920.8 times lower than in China ($464.2 billion), 595.1 times lower than in Germany ($300.0 billion), and 511.2 times lower than in the United Kingdom ($257.7 billion). The value of transportation per capita in Brunei was 3.7 times higher than in China ($331.0); but 4.6 times lower than in the USA ($5.6 thousand), 3.4 times lower than in Japan ($4.1 thousand), 3.2 times lower than in the United Kingdom ($3.9 thousand), and 3.0 times lower than in Germany ($3.7 thousand). The growth of transportation in Brunei was greater than in the UK (2.8%), in Germany (2.7%), and in Japan (0.81%); but less than in China (7.5%) and in the United States (5.1%).

Chapter VIII. Trade

Wholesale, retail trade, restaurants and hotels (ISIC G-H)

The sector of trade in Brunei rose from $33.1 million per year in the 1970s to $800.4 million per year in the 2010s, that is by $767.3 million or 24.2 times. The change occurred at $568.1 million due to a 3.4-fold increase in prices, as also at $146.3 million due to a 2.7-fold increase in productivity, as well as at $52.9 million due to the expansion in population. The average annual growth in trade is 8.4%. The minimum value of trade was in 1970 at $2.0 million. The maximum value of trade was in 2013 at $908.2 million.

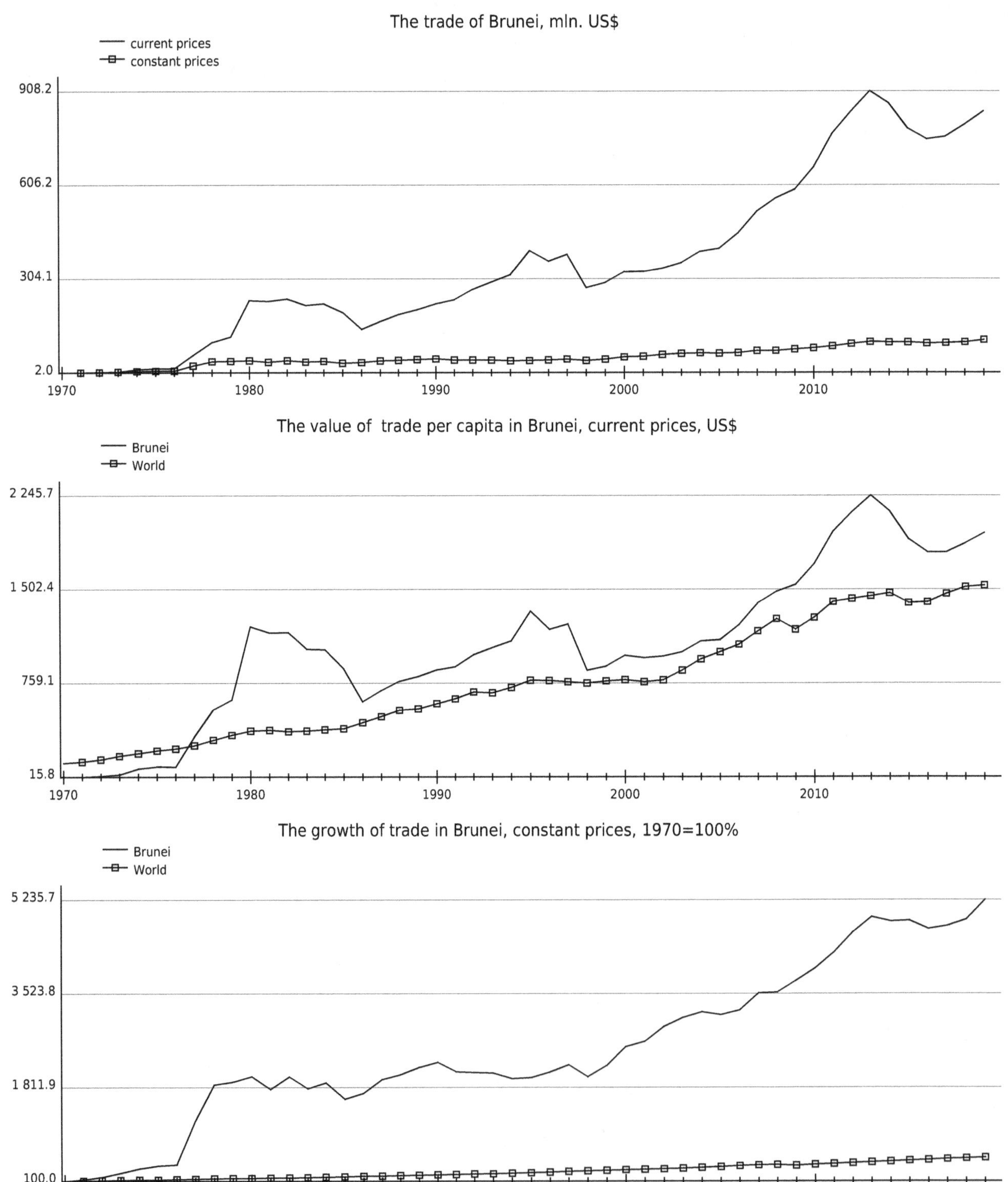

The trade of Brunei, mln. US$

The value of trade per capita in Brunei, current prices, US$

The growth of trade in Brunei, constant prices, 1970=100%

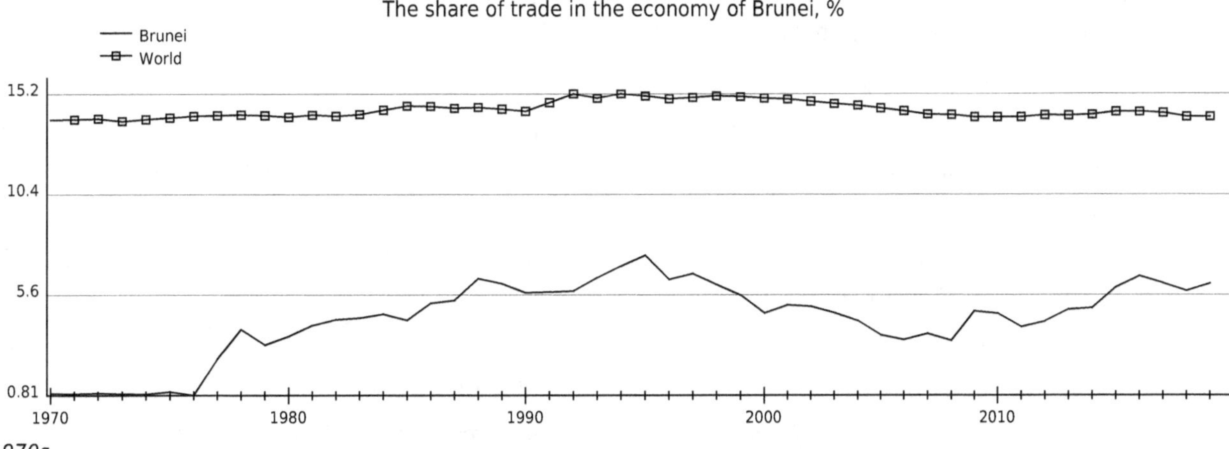

The 1970s

The trade of Brunei was $33.1 million per year in the 1970s, ranked 149th in the world, and was on a par with Burundi ($33.6 million). The share in the world was 0.0037%, and 0.021% in Asia.

The share of trade in the economy of Brunei was 2.3% in the 1970s, ranked 184th in the world.

The trade per capita in Brunei was $209.0 in the 1970s, ranked 67th in the world, and was on a par with Melanesia ($206.7), Eastern Europe ($212.7), Gabon ($213.2). The value of trade per capita in Brunei was less than trade per capita in the world ($221.0) by 5.5%, and was greater than trade per capita in Asia ($67.4) in 3.1 times.

The growth of trade in Brunei was 38.8% in the 1970s, ranked 1st in the world. The growth of trade in Brunei (38.8%) was greater than growth of trade in the world (4.5%), was greater than growth of trade in Asia (7.7%).

Comparison with neighbors. The trade of Brunei was less than in Malaysia ($1.1 billion). The trade per capita in Brunei was greater than in Malaysia ($87.7). The growth of trade in Brunei was greater than in Malaysia (10.7%).

Comparison with leaders. The value added of trade in Brunei was less than in the United States ($278.3 billion), in Japan ($90.3 billion), in the USSR ($62.3 billion), in Germany ($61.1 billion), and in France ($40.9 billion). The value of trade per capita in Brunei was less than in the USA ($1 275.1), in Japan ($811.1), in Germany ($775.5), in France ($762.4), and in the USSR ($247.1). The growth of trade in Brunei was greater than in Japan (8.2%), in the USSR (5.2%), in France (3.9%), in the United States (3.9%), and in Germany (3.0%).

The 1980s

The sector of trade in Brunei was $204.2 million per year in the 1980s, ranked 126th in the world, and was on a par with Andorra ($206.6 million), Suriname ($199.3 million). The share in the world was 0.0097%, and 0.043% in Asia.

The share of trade in the economy of Brunei was 4.7% in the 1980s, ranked 184th in the world.

The trade per capita in Brunei was $920.3 in the 1980s, ranked 48th in the world, and was on a par with Europe ($921.4), Israel ($899.2). The value of trade per capita in Brunei was greater than trade per capita in the world ($437.7) in 2.1 times, and was greater than trade per capita in Asia ($166.8) in 5.5 times.

The growth of trade in Brunei was 1.3% in the 1980s, ranked 138th in the world, and was on a par with Bermuda (1.3%). The growth of trade in Brunei (1.3%) was less than growth of trade in the world (3.3%), was less than growth of trade in Asia (5.8%).

Comparison with neighbors. The sector of trade in Brunei was less than in Malaysia ($3.4 billion). The Brunei's trade per capita was greater than in Malaysia ($218.5). The growth of trade in Brunei was less than in Malaysia (5.1%).

Comparison with leaders. The trade of Brunei was less than in the United States ($653.3 billion), in Japan ($277.3 billion), in Germany ($116.7 billion), in the USSR ($112.3 billion), and in Italy ($95.7 billion). The value of trade per capita in Brunei was greater than in the USSR ($408.1); but less than in the United States ($2.7 thousand), in Japan ($2.3 thousand), in Italy ($1 684.2), and in Germany ($1 496.0). The growth of trade in Brunei was greater than in the USSR (-0.62%); but less than in Japan (4.9%), in the USA (4.4%), in Italy (2.3%), and in Germany (1.8%).

The 1990s

The sector of trade in Brunei was $304.3 million per year in the 1990s, ranked 147th in the world, and was on a par with Liechtenstein ($301.2 million). The share in the world was 0.0074%, and 0.026% in Asia.

The share of trade in the economy of Brunei was 6.3% in the 1990s, ranked 203rd in the world.

The value added of trade per capita in Brunei was $1 038.8 in the 1990s, ranked 59th in the world, and was on a par with Slovenia ($1 042.7). The sector of trade per capita in Brunei was greater than trade per capita in the world ($721.8) by 43.9%, and was greater than trade per capita in Asia ($337.1) in 3.1 times.

The growth of trade in Brunei was 0.2% in the 1990s, ranked 162nd in the world. The growth of trade in Brunei (0.16%) was less than growth of trade in the world (3.5%), was less than growth of trade in Asia (4.9%).

Comparison with neighbors. The value of trade in Brunei was less than in Malaysia ($10.9 billion). The trade per capita in Brunei was greater than in Malaysia ($539.4). The growth of trade in Brunei was less than in Malaysia (9.3%).

Comparison with leaders. The sector of trade in Brunei was less than in the United States ($1.2 trillion), in Japan ($713.2 billion), in Germany ($243.7 billion), in Italy ($185.6 billion), and in France ($177.0 billion). The trade per capita in Brunei was less than in Japan ($5.7 thousand), in the USA ($4.4 thousand), in Italy ($3.3 thousand), in Germany ($3.0 thousand), and in France ($3.0 thousand). The growth of trade in Brunei was less than in the USA (4.3%), in Japan (3.8%), in Germany (2.5%), in France (2.4%), and in Italy (1.9%).

The 2000s

The value of trade in Brunei was $426.5 million per year in the 2000s, ranked 157th in the world, and was on a par with Gambia ($429.2 million), Suriname ($433.0 million). The share in the world was 0.0066%, and 0.025% in Asia.

The share of trade in the economy of Brunei was 4.2% in the 2000s, ranked 209th in the world.

The value added of trade per capita in Brunei was $1 182.7 in the 2000s, ranked 71st in the world, and was on a par with Oman ($1 194.3), Central America ($1 205.2). The value of trade per capita in Brunei was greater than trade per capita in the world ($990.3) by 19.4%, and was greater than trade per capita in Asia ($438.7) in 2.7 times.

The growth of trade in Brunei was 5.5% in the 2000s, ranked 73rd in the world, and was on a par with Lithuania (5.4%), Oman (5.5%). The growth of trade in Brunei (5.5%) was greater than growth of trade in the world (2.7%), was greater than growth of trade in Asia (4.5%).

Comparison with neighbors. The sector of trade in Brunei was less than in Malaysia ($20.5 billion). The sector of trade per capita in Brunei was greater than in Malaysia ($806.3). The growth of trade in Brunei was less than in Malaysia (6.5%).

Comparison with leaders. The value added of trade in Brunei was less than in the USA ($1.9 trillion), in Japan ($771.8 billion), in Germany ($296.0 billion), in the United Kingdom ($293.5 billion), and in China ($262.0 billion). The trade per capita in Brunei was greater than in China ($197.5); but less than in the United States ($6.4 thousand), in Japan ($6.0 thousand), in the United Kingdom ($4.9 thousand), and in Germany ($3.6 thousand). The growth of trade in Brunei was greater than in Germany (1.7%), in the UK (1.3%), in the USA (1.1%), and in Japan (-0.77%); but less than in China (11.9%).

The 2010s

The sector of trade in Brunei was $800.4 million per year in the 2010s, ranked 157th in the world, and was on a par with Gabon ($804.7 million). The share in the world was 0.0076%, and 0.022% in Asia.

The share of trade in the economy of Brunei was 5.2% in the 2010s, ranked 206th in the world, and was on a par with Gabon (5.3%).

The trade per capita in Brunei was $1 944.3 in the 2010s, ranked 73rd in the world, and was on a par with Malaysia ($1 929.6), Venezuela ($1 968.1), Mexico ($1 970.5). The trade per capita in Brunei was greater than trade per capita in the world ($1 436.8) by 35.3%, and was greater than trade per capita in Asia ($821.1) in 2.4 times.

The growth of trade in Brunei was 3.4% in the 2010s, ranked 110th in the world. The growth of trade in Brunei (3.4%) was greater than growth of trade in the world (3.3%), was less than growth of trade in Asia (5.6%).

Comparison with neighbors. The value added of trade in Brunei was 72.5 times lower than in Malaysia ($58.0 billion). The sector of trade per capita in Brunei was 0.76% higher than in Malaysia ($1 929.6). The growth of trade in Brunei was less than in Malaysia (7.0%).

Comparison with leaders. The Brunei's trade was 3 267.5 times lower than in the United States ($2.6 trillion), 1 492.2 times lower than in China ($1.2 trillion), 1 086.3 times lower than in Japan ($869.5 billion), 465.5 times lower than in Germany ($372.6 billion), and 412.2 times lower than in the UK ($330.0 billion). The Brunei's trade per capita was 2.3 times higher than in China ($851.7); but 4.2 times lower than in the United States ($8.2 thousand), 3.5 times lower than in Japan ($6.8 thousand), 2.6 times lower than in the United Kingdom ($5.0 thousand), and 2.3 times lower than in Germany ($4.6 thousand). The growth of trade in Brunei was greater than in the United Kingdom (2.8%), in the USA (2.3%), in Germany (2.0%), and in Japan (0.77%); but less than in China (8.9%).

Chapter IX. Services

(ISIC J-P)

The sector of services in Brunei rose from $96.9 million per year in the 1970s to $3.8 billion per year in the 2010s, that is by $3.7 billion or 39.5 times. The change occurred at $2.9 billion due to a 4.2-fold increase in prices, as also at $660.9 million due to a 3.6-fold increase in productivity, as well as at $154.9 million due to the expansion in population. The average annual growth in services is 6.6%. The minimum value of services was in 1970 at $13.0 million. The maximum value of services was in 2014 at $4.2 billion.

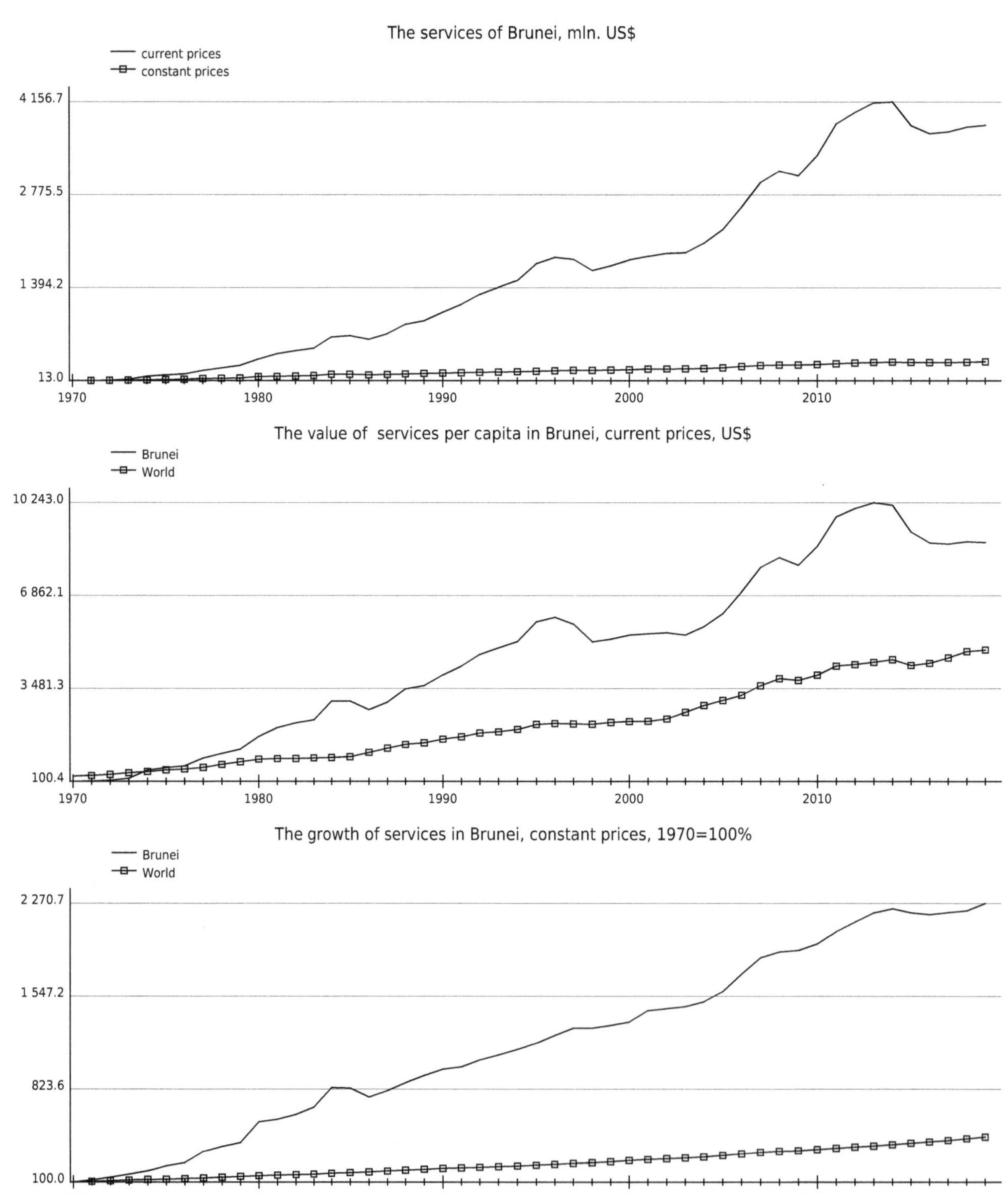

The services of Brunei, mln. US$

The value of services per capita in Brunei, current prices, US$

The growth of services in Brunei, constant prices, 1970=100%

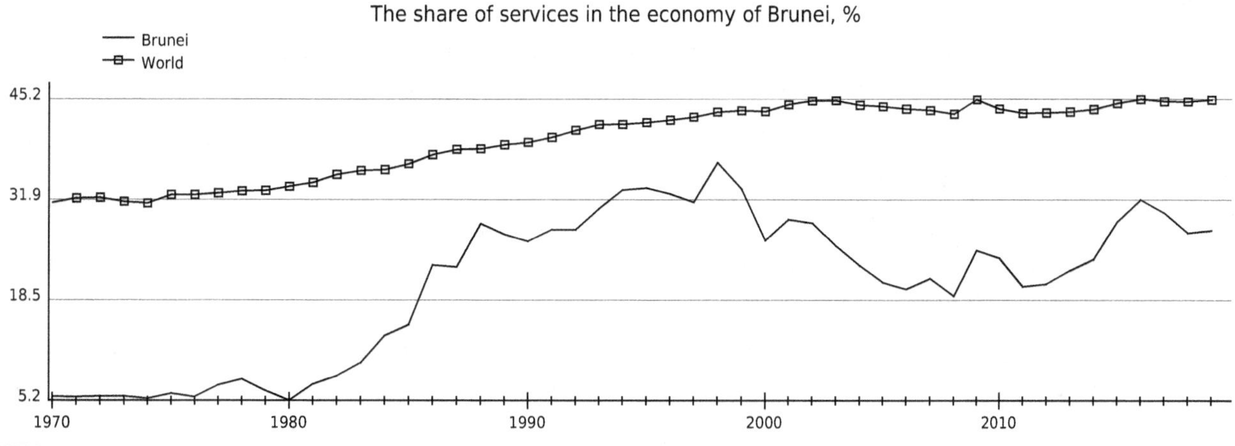

The 1970s

The services of Brunei were $96.9 million per year in the 1970s, ranked 140th in the world, and were on a par with Greenland ($96.7 million), Eswatini ($97.7 million). The share in the world was 0.0047%, and 0.034% in Asia.

The share of services in the economy of Brunei was 6.6% in the 1970s, ranked 185th in the world.

The value of services per capita in Brunei was $611.6 in the 1970s, ranked 54th in the world. The Brunei's services per capita were greater than services per capita in the world ($506.9) by 20.7%, and were greater than services per capita in Asia ($121.6) in 5.0 times.

The growth of services in Brunei was 16.9% in the 1970s, ranked 1st in the world. The growth of services in Brunei (16.9%) was greater than growth of services in the world (4.1%), was greater than growth of services in Asia (6.5%).

Comparison with neighbors. The Brunei's services were less than in Malaysia ($2.1 billion). The Brunei's services per capita were greater than in Malaysia ($171.9). The growth of services in Brunei was greater than in Malaysia (9.5%).

Comparison with leaders. The value added of services in Brunei was less than in the USA ($674.4 billion), in the USSR ($168.3 billion), in Japan ($153.8 billion), in Germany ($150.2 billion), and in France ($121.8 billion). The Brunei's services per capita were less than in the USA ($3.1 thousand), in France ($2.3 thousand), in Germany ($1 907.6), in Japan ($1 381.3), and in the USSR ($667.3). The growth of services in Brunei was greater than in Japan (5.9%), in Germany (4.8%), in France (3.9%), in the United States (3.3%), and in the USSR (0.90%).

The 1980s

The value added of services in Brunei was $611.9 million per year in the 1980s, ranked 113th in the world, and was on a par with Myanmar ($607.6 million). The share in the world was 0.011%, and 0.061% in Asia.

The share of services in the economy of Brunei was 14.1% in the 1980s, ranked 175th in the world, and was on a par with Malawi (14.1%).

The Brunei's services per capita were $2 757.5 in the 1980s, ranked 39th in the world. The Brunei's services per capita were greater than services per capita in the world ($1 115.5) in 2.5 times, and were greater than services per capita in Asia ($351.5) in 7.8 times.

The growth of services in Brunei was 8.6% in the 1980s, ranked 16th in the world, and was on a par with the UAE (8.7%), the Cook Islands (8.7%). The growth of services in Brunei (8.6%) was greater than growth of services in the world (3.3%), was greater than growth of services in Asia (5.3%).

Comparison with neighbors. The Brunei's services were less than in Malaysia ($7.2 billion). The Brunei's services per capita were greater than in Malaysia ($464.2). The growth of services in Brunei was greater than in Malaysia (6.2%).

Comparison with leaders. The value added of services in Brunei was less than in the United States ($1.9 trillion), in Japan ($619.9 billion), in Germany ($362.2 billion), in France ($294.5 billion), and in the UK ($265.4 billion). The Brunei's services per capita were less than in the USA ($7.8 thousand), in France ($5.2 thousand), in Japan ($5.1 thousand), in the United Kingdom ($4.7 thousand), and in Germany ($4.6 thousand). The growth of services in Brunei was greater than in Japan (4.8%), in the United Kingdom (3.3%), in Germany (3.1%), in the USA (2.8%), and in France (2.3%).

The 1990s

The sector of services in Brunei was $1.5 billion per year in the 1990s, ranked 111th in the world, and was on a par with Macedonia ($1.5 billion), Latvia ($1.5 billion), New Caledonia ($1.5 billion). The share in the world was 0.013%, and 0.060% in Asia.

The share of services in the economy of Brunei was 31.5% in the 1990s, ranked 104th in the world, and was on a par with Burkina Faso (31.5%), Serbia (31.6%), Morocco (31.4%).

The services per capita in Brunei were $5 171.1 in the 1990s, ranked 40th in the world, and were on a par with Europe ($5.3 thousand). The Brunei's services per capita were greater than services per capita in the world ($2 014.6) in 2.6 times, and were greater than services per capita in Asia ($732.9) in 7.1 times.

The growth of services in Brunei was 3.6% in the 1990s, ranked 77th in the world, and was on a par with the Solomon Islands (3.5%). The growth of services in Brunei (3.6%) was greater than growth of services in the world (2.7%), was less than growth of services in Asia (4.5%).

Comparison with neighbors. The value added of services in Brunei was less than in Malaysia ($19.1 billion). The services per capita in Brunei were greater than in Malaysia ($942.8). The growth of services in Brunei was less than in Malaysia (7.9%).

Comparison with leaders. The sector of services in Brunei was less than in the USA ($3.8 trillion), in Japan ($1.6 trillion), in Germany ($908.0 billion), in France ($628.2 billion), and in the UK ($592.3 billion). The value added of services per capita in Brunei was less than in the USA ($14.4 thousand), in Japan ($12.8 thousand), in Germany ($11.3 thousand), in France ($10.6 thousand), and in the United Kingdom ($10.2 thousand). The growth of services in Brunei was greater than in Germany (3.2%), in the UK (3.0%), in the USA (2.3%), in Japan (1.7%), and in France (1.6%).

The 2000s

The sector of services in Brunei was $2.4 billion per year in the 2000s, ranked 119th in the world, and was on a par with Azerbaijan ($2.4 billion), Namibia ($2.4 billion). The share in the world was 0.012%, and 0.056% in Asia.

The share of services in the economy of Brunei was 23.0% in the 2000s, ranked 171st in the world, and was on a par with Laos (23.0%), Northern Africa (23.0%), Vietnam (23.0%).

The services per capita in Brunei were $6 530.1 in the 2000s, ranked 49th in the world. The value added of services per capita in Brunei was greater than services per capita in the world ($3 011.2) in 2.2 times, and was greater than services per capita in Asia ($1 071.6) in 6.1 times.

The growth of services in Brunei was 3.7% in the 2000s, ranked 116th in the world, and was on a par with Somalia (3.7%), Bosnia and Herzegovina (3.7%), Ireland (3.7%). The growth of services in Brunei (3.7%) was greater than growth of services in the world (2.9%), was less than growth of services in Asia (5.5%).

Comparison with neighbors. The services of Brunei were less than in Malaysia ($36.3 billion). The value of services per capita in Brunei was greater than in Malaysia ($1 427.7). The growth of services in Brunei was less than in Malaysia (6.1%).

Comparison with leaders. The Brunei's services were less than in the USA ($6.7 trillion), in Japan ($2.0 trillion), in Germany ($1.2 trillion), in the United Kingdom ($1.1 trillion), and in France ($997.0 billion). The value of services per capita in Brunei was less than in the United States ($22.9 thousand), in the UK ($18.0 thousand), in France ($15.9 thousand), in Japan ($15.3 thousand), and in Germany ($15.0 thousand). The growth of services in Brunei was greater than in the UK (2.7%), in the USA (2.0%), in France (1.5%), in Japan (1.2%), and in Germany (0.57%).

The 2010s

The sector of services in Brunei was $3.8 billion per year in the 2010s, ranked 129th in the world. The share in the world was 0.012%, and 0.041% in Asia.

The share of services in the economy of Brunei was 25.1% in the 2010s, ranked 170th in the world, and was on a par with Vietnam (25.0%), South Sudan (24.9%).

The sector of services per capita in Brunei was $9 301.1 in the 2010s, ranked 49th in the world. The services per capita in Brunei were greater than services per capita in the world ($4 467.8) in 2.1 times, and were greater than services per capita in Asia ($2 137.6) in 4.4 times.

The growth of services in Brunei was 1.8% in the 2010s, ranked 143rd in the world, and was on a par with the United States (1.8%), the Cayman Islands (1.8%), Bosnia and Herzegovina (1.8%). The growth of services in Brunei (1.8%) was less than growth of services in the world (2.7%), was less than growth of services in Asia (5.4%).

Comparison with neighbors. The sector of services in Brunei was 19.9 times lower than in Malaysia ($76.3 billion). The services per capita in Brunei were 3.7 times higher than in Malaysia ($2.5 thousand). The growth of services in Brunei was less than in Malaysia (5.6%).

Comparison with leaders. The value added of services in Brunei was 2 599.8 times lower than in the United States ($10.0 trillion), 926.3 times lower than in China ($3.5 trillion), 593.7 times lower than in Japan ($2.3 trillion), 419.8 times lower than in Germany ($1.6 trillion), and 354.0 times lower than in the UK ($1.4 trillion). The services per capita in Brunei were 3.7 times higher than in China ($2.5 thousand); but 3.4 times lower than in the United States ($31.2 thousand), 2.2 times lower than in the UK ($20.7 thousand), 2.1 times lower than in Germany ($19.6 thousand), and 47.7% lower than in Japan ($17.8 thousand). The growth of services in Brunei was greater than in the USA (1.8%), in the United Kingdom (1.7%), in Germany (1.2%), and in Japan (0.99%); but less than in China (8.4%).

Part III. External relations

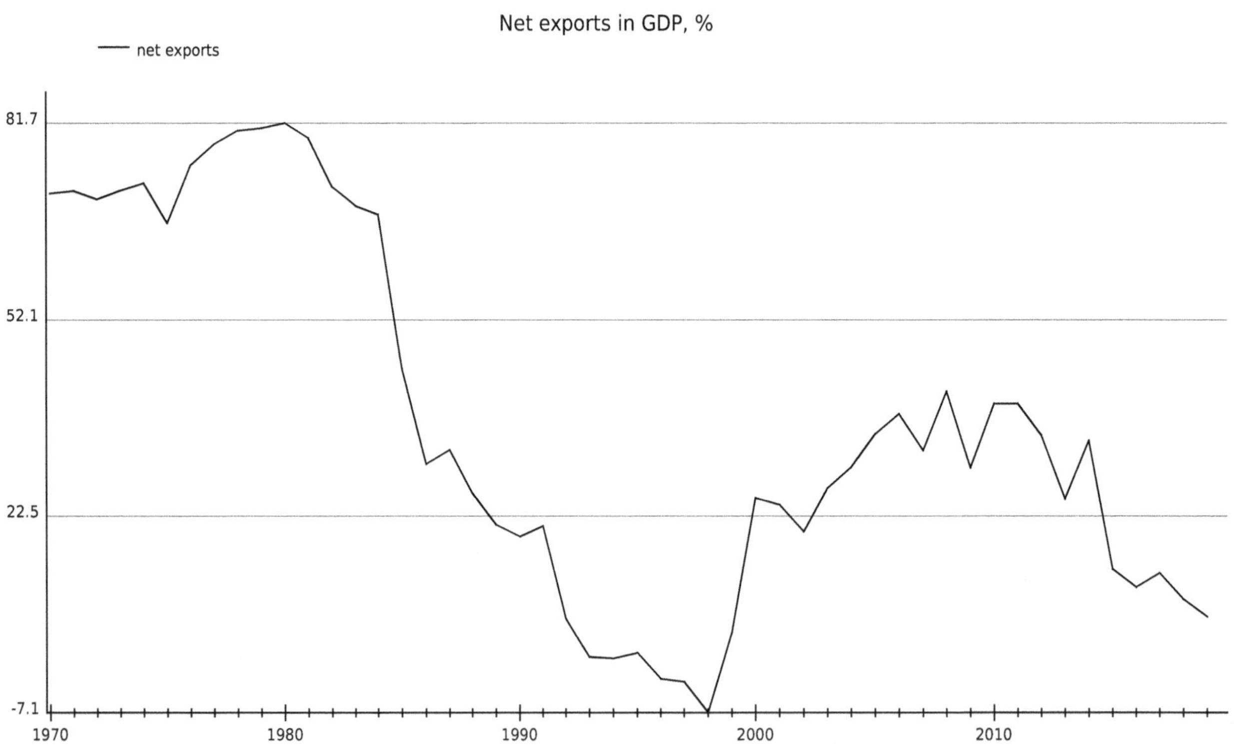

Chapter X. Exports

Exports of goods and services

The value of exports from Brunei increased from $1.3 billion per year in the 1970s to $9.3 billion per year in the 2010s, that is by $8.0 billion or 7.0 times. The change occurred at $7.8 billion due to a 6.3-fold increase in prices, as also at -$1.9 billion due to a 2.3-fold decrease in per capita rate, as well as at $2.1 billion due to the growing in population. The average annual growth in exports is 1.3%. The minimum value of exports was in 1970 at $204.2 million. The maximum value of exports was in 2012 at $13.4 billion.

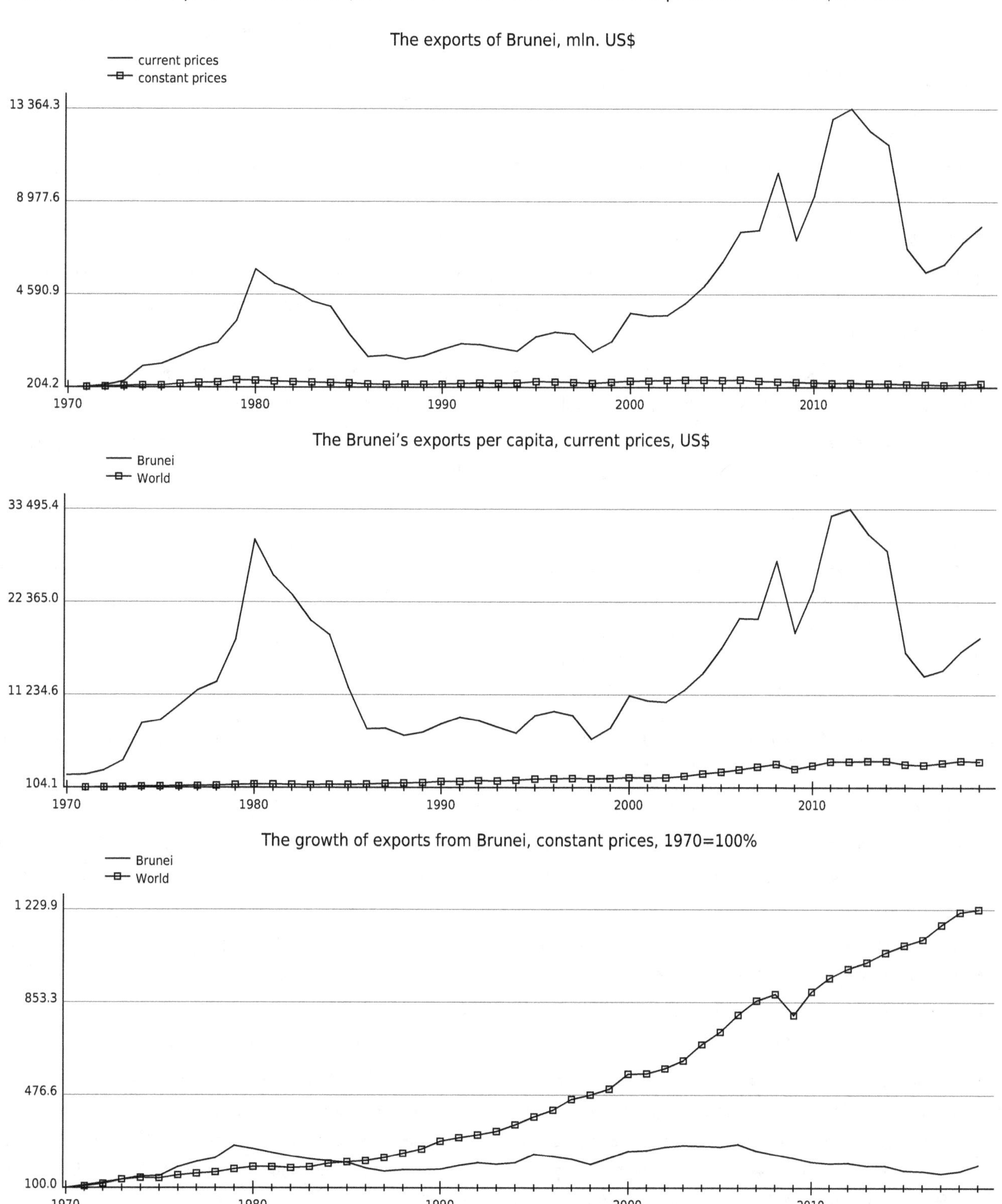

The 1970s

The value of exports from Brunei was $1.3 billion per year in the 1970s, ranked 66th in the world, and was on a par with Zambia ($1.3 billion). The share in the world was 0.13%, and 0.62% from Asia.

The share of exports in GDP of Brunei was 93.4% in the 1970s, ranked 5th in the world, and was on a par with Aruba (93.0%).

The exports per capita from Brunei were $8 311.9 in the 1970s, ranked 4th in the world, and were on a par with Kuwait ($8.2 thousand), Luxembourg ($8.2 thousand). The value of exports per capita from Brunei was greater than exports per capita in the world ($242.1) in 34.3 times, and was greater than exports per capita from Asia ($90.8) in 91.5 times.

The growth of exports from Brunei was 11.7% in the 1970s, ranked 21st in the world. The growth of exports from Brunei (11.7%) was greater than growth of exports in the world (6.5%), was greater than growth of exports from Asia (7.9%).

Comparison with neighbors. The value of exports from Brunei was less than from Malaysia ($5.0 billion). The value of exports per capita from Brunei was greater than from Malaysia ($410.6). The growth of exports from Brunei was greater than from Malaysia (11.0%).

Comparison with leaders. The Brunei's exports were less than from the USA ($128.0 billion), from Germany ($82.9 billion), from France ($64.3 billion), from Japan ($64.1 billion), and from the United Kingdom ($61.3 billion). The exports per capita from Brunei were greater than from France ($1 199.1), from the United Kingdom ($1 094.1), from Germany ($1 052.2), from the United States ($586.5), and from Japan ($575.8). The growth of exports from Brunei was greater than from Japan (8.6%), from France (7.8%), from the United States (6.8%), from Germany (5.1%), and from the United Kingdom (5.0%).

The 1980s

The Brunei's exports were $3.3 billion per year in the 1980s, ranked 64th in the world, and were on a par with Tunisia ($3.3 billion). The share in the world was 0.13%, and 0.51% from Asia.

The share of exports in GDP of Brunei was 77.2% in the 1980s, ranked 10th in the world.

The value of exports per capita from Brunei was $14 987.4 in the 1980s, ranked 5th in the world, and was on a par with Liechtenstein ($15.1 thousand). The Brunei's exports per capita were greater than exports per capita in the world ($529.9) in 28.3 times, and were greater than exports per capita from Asia ($229.0) in 65.4 times.

The growth of exports from Brunei was -4.4% in the 1980s, ranked 174th in the world. The growth of exports from Brunei (-4.4%) was less than growth of exports in the world (3.8%), was less than growth of exports from Asia (4.1%).

Comparison with neighbors. The Brunei's exports were less than from Malaysia ($17.9 billion). The value of exports per capita from Brunei was greater than from Malaysia ($1 153.9). The growth of exports from Brunei was less than from Malaysia (9.4%).

Comparison with leaders. The exports of Brunei were less than from the United States ($338.6 billion), from Japan ($210.6 billion), from Germany ($208.1 billion), from France ($155.9 billion), and from the United Kingdom ($155.0 billion). The value of exports per capita from Brunei was greater than from France ($2.8 thousand), from the UK ($2.7 thousand), from Germany ($2.7 thousand), from Japan ($1 736.5), and from the USA ($1 413.8). The growth of exports from Brunei was less than from Japan (6.7%), from the United States (5.7%), from Germany (4.7%), from France (4.0%), and from the UK (3.0%).

The 1990s

The value of exports from Brunei was $2.3 billion per year in the 1990s, ranked 107th in the world, and was on a par with the Bahamas ($2.3 billion), Mauritius ($2.3 billion), Botswana ($2.3 billion). The share in the world was 0.039%, and 0.14% from Asia.

The share of exports in GDP of Brunei was 47.6% in the 1990s, ranked 51st in the world, and was on a par with Greenland (47.5%), the Caribbean (47.7%), Gambia (47.2%).

The exports per capita from Brunei were $7 790.2 in the 1990s, ranked 29th in the world, and were on a par with Finland ($7.8 thousand), the Turks and Caicos Islands ($7.7 thousand), Western Europe ($7.9 thousand). The value of exports per capita from Brunei was greater than exports per capita in the world ($1 029.5) in 7.6 times, and was greater than exports per capita from Asia ($456.7) in 17.1 times.

The growth of exports from Brunei was 2.5% in the 1990s, ranked 145th in the world, and was on a par with Africa (2.5%). The growth of exports from Brunei (2.5%) was less than growth of exports in the world (6.9%), was less than growth of exports from Asia (8.1%).

Comparison with neighbors. The value of exports from Brunei was less than from Malaysia ($68.4 billion). The Brunei's exports per capita were greater than from Malaysia ($3.4 thousand). The growth of exports from Brunei was less than from Malaysia (12.5%).

Comparison with leaders. The Brunei's exports were less than from the USA ($773.6 billion), from Germany ($509.0 billion), from Japan ($418.7 billion), from France ($329.8 billion), and from the UK ($324.3 billion). The Brunei's exports per capita were greater than from Germany ($6.3 thousand), from the United Kingdom ($5.6 thousand), from France ($5.6 thousand), from Japan ($3.3 thousand), and from the USA ($2.9 thousand). The growth of exports from Brunei was less than from the United States (7.2%), from France (6.5%), from Germany (6.0%), from the UK (5.7%), and from Japan (4.2%).

The 2000s

The exports of Brunei were $5.9 billion per year in the 2000s, ranked 97th in the world. The share in the world was 0.047%, and 0.15% from Asia.

The structure of exports: primary products (93.2%), low technology manufactures (4.0%), and medium technology manufactures (1.3%).

Brunei exported goods to Japan (39.4%), South Korea (13.5%), Indonesia (12.4%), Australia (9.7%), the United States (5.5%) and other countries (19.5%).

The share of exports in GDP of Brunei was 58.8% in the 2000s, ranked 43rd in the world, and was on a par with Czechia (58.6%), Azerbaijan (59.0%), Belarus (58.4%).

The exports per capita from Brunei were $16 307.7 in the 2000s, ranked 27th in the world, and were on a par with Iceland ($16.5 thousand). The exports per capita from Brunei were greater than exports per capita in the world ($1 933.7) in 8.4 times, and were greater than exports per capita from Asia ($1 011.8) in 16.1 times.

The growth of exports from Brunei was 0% in the 2000s, ranked 184th in the world. The growth of exports from Brunei (0.0032%) was less than growth of exports in the world (4.8%), was less than growth of exports from Asia (7.5%).

Comparison with neighbors. The Brunei's exports were less than from Malaysia ($155.0 billion). The exports per capita from Brunei were greater than from Malaysia ($6.1 thousand). The growth of exports from Brunei was less than from Malaysia (4.2%).

Comparison with leaders. The Brunei's exports were less than from the USA ($1.3 trillion), from Germany ($1.0 trillion), from China ($780.2 billion), from Japan ($626.3 billion), and from the UK ($591.1 billion). The exports per capita from Brunei were greater than from Germany ($12.8 thousand), from the United Kingdom ($9.8 thousand), from Japan ($4.9 thousand), from the USA ($4.5 thousand), and from China ($588.1). The growth of exports from Brunei was less than from China (12.7%), from Germany (5.0%), from Japan (3.5%), from the USA (3.3%), and from the United Kingdom (2.8%).

The 2010s

The Brunei's exports were $9.3 billion per year in the 2010s, ranked 107th in the world, and were on a par with Honduras ($9.3 billion), Zambia ($9.2 billion), Iceland ($9.5 billion). The share in the world was 0.041%, and 0.11% from Asia.

The structure of exports: primary products (94.7%) and medium technology manufactures (3.0%).

Brunei exported goods to Japan (40.3%), South Korea (14.7%), Australia (7.9%), India (7.6%), Thailand (5.4%) and other countries (24.1%).

The share of exports in GDP of Brunei was 61.8% in the 2010s, ranked 42nd in the world, and was on a par with Qatar (61.6%), South-Eastern Asia (62.4%).

The exports per capita from Brunei were $22 520.4 in the 2010s, ranked 26th in the world, and were on a par with Western Europe ($22.7 thousand), Puerto Rico ($22.8 thousand). The Brunei's exports per capita were greater than exports per capita in the world ($3 098.9) in 7.3 times, and were greater than exports per capita from Asia ($1 964.3) in 11.5 times.

The growth of exports from Brunei was -1.4% in the 2010s, ranked 194th in the world. The growth of exports from Brunei (-1.4%) was less than growth of exports in the world (4.4%), was less than growth of exports from Asia (5.3%).

Comparison with neighbors. The exports of Brunei were 25.2 times lower than from Malaysia ($233.7 billion). The Brunei's exports per capita were 2.9 times higher than from Malaysia ($7.8 thousand). The growth of exports from Brunei was less than from Malaysia (2.9%).

Comparison with leaders. The exports of Brunei were 247.4 times lower than from China ($2.3 trillion), 244.8 times lower than from the United States ($2.3 trillion), 181.6 times lower than from Germany ($1.7 trillion), 92.7 times lower than from Japan ($859.4 billion), and 87.9 times lower than from the UK ($815.1 billion). The Brunei's exports per capita were 9.5% higher than from Germany ($20.6 thousand), 81.2% higher than from the UK ($12.4 thousand), 3.2 times higher than from the USA ($7.1 thousand), 3.4 times higher than from Japan ($6.7 thousand), and 13.8 times higher than from China ($1 635.3). The growth of exports from Brunei was less than from China (6.8%), from Germany (4.7%), from Japan (4.6%), from the United States (3.7%), and from the United Kingdom (3.1%).

Chapter XI. Imports

Imports of goods and services

The Brunei's imports grew up from $237.3 million per year in the 1970s to $5.6 billion per year in the 2010s, that is by $5.3 billion or 23.5 times. The change occurred at $4.2 billion due to a 4.0-fold increase in prices, as also at $791.6 million due to a 2.3-fold increase in per capita rate, as well as at $379.3 million due to the rise in population. The average annual growth in imports is 4.9%. The minimum value of imports was in 1970 at $44.2 million. The maximum value of imports was in 2013 at $7.8 billion.

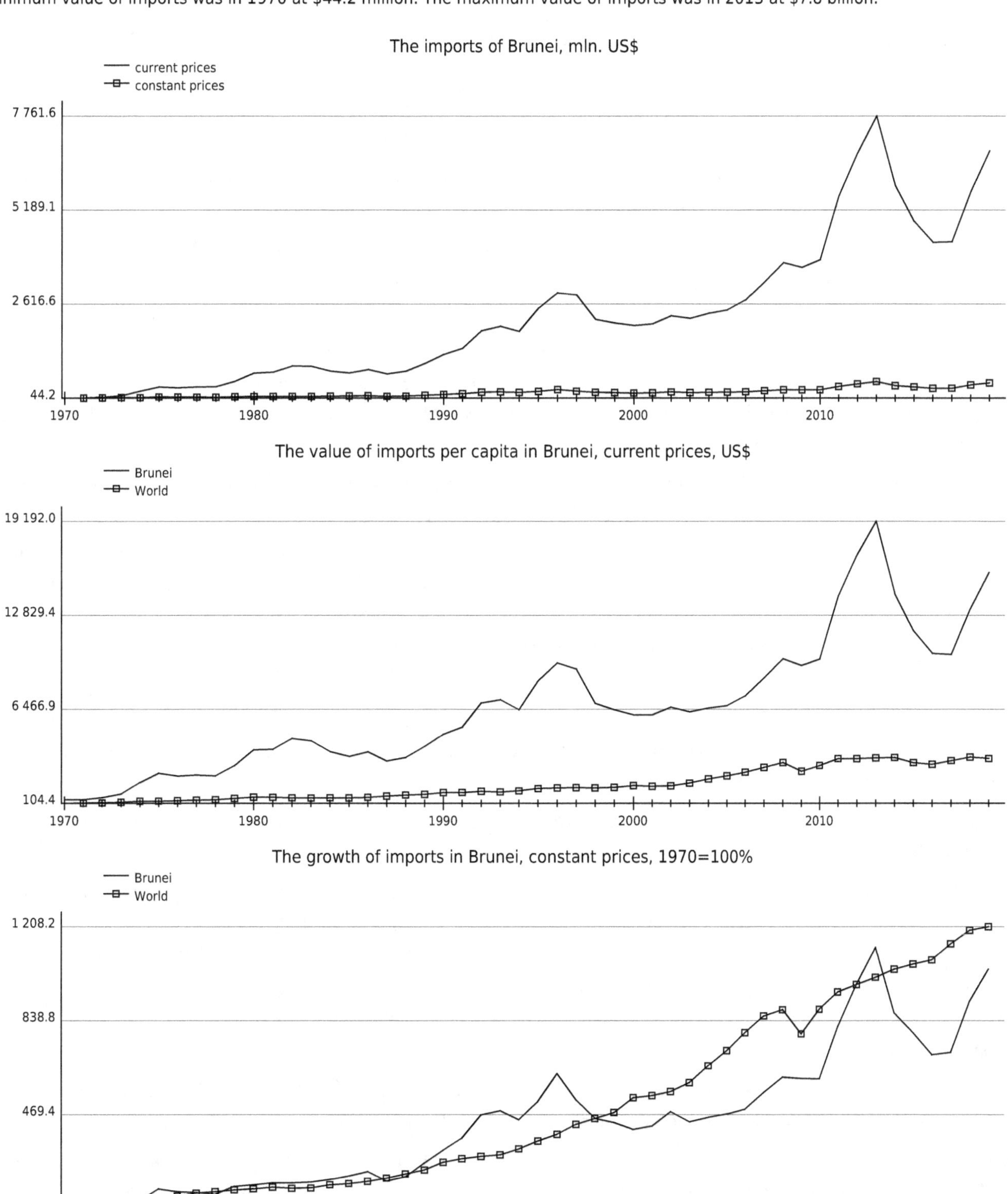

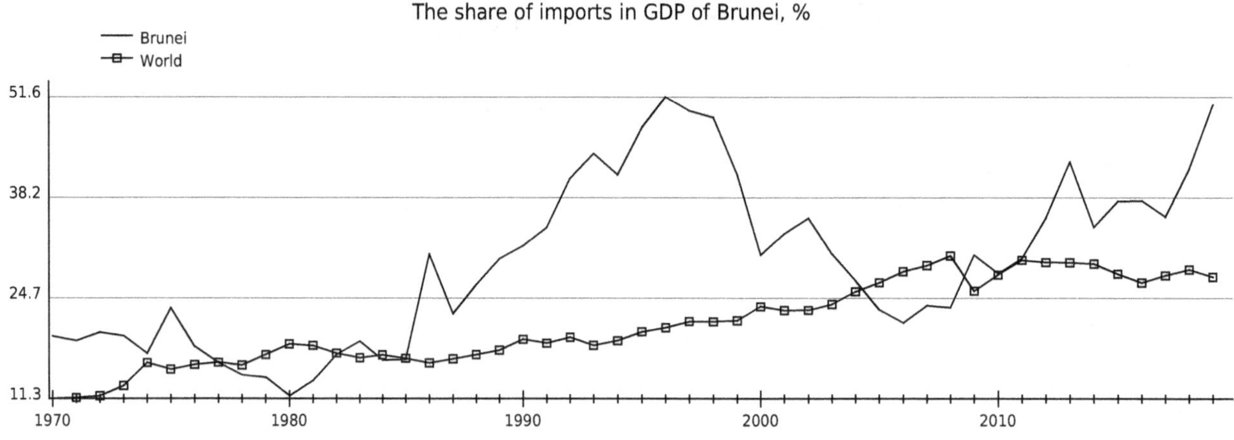

The 1970s

The Brunei's imports were $237.3 million per year in the 1970s, ranked 131st in the world, and were on a par with Mali ($241.2 million), El Salvador ($231.7 million). The share in the world was 0.024%, and 0.13% in Asia.

The share of imports in GDP of Brunei was 16.8% in the 1970s, ranked 157th in the world, and was on a par with Oceania (16.9%).

The value of imports per capita in Brunei was $1 497.8 in the 1970s, ranked 37th in the world, and was on a par with Cyprus ($1 510.3), Ireland ($1 527.7). The value of imports per capita in Brunei was greater than imports per capita in the world ($244.3) in 6.1 times, and was greater than imports per capita in Asia ($79.6) in 18.8 times.

The growth of imports in Brunei was 7.2% in the 1970s, ranked 69th in the world, and was on a par with Thailand (7.1%), France (7.2%), the Philippines (7.2%). The growth of imports in Brunei (7.2%) was greater than growth of imports in the world (6.3%), was less than growth of imports in Asia (9.6%).

Comparison with neighbors. The imports of Brunei were less than in Malaysia ($4.4 billion). The imports per capita in Brunei were greater than in Malaysia ($364.3). The growth of imports in Brunei was less than in Malaysia (12.0%).

Comparison with leaders. The value of imports in Brunei was less than in the United States ($133.2 billion), in Germany ($92.5 billion), in France ($63.3 billion), in the United Kingdom ($62.4 billion), and in Japan ($61.0 billion). The value of imports per capita in Brunei was greater than in France ($1 181.1), in Germany ($1 175.1), in the United Kingdom ($1 113.2), in the USA ($610.4), and in Japan ($547.6). The growth of imports in Brunei was greater than in France (7.2%), in Japan (7.0%), in Germany (5.6%), in the USA (5.1%), and in the UK (4.5%).

The 1980s

The imports of Brunei were $813.2 million per year in the 1980s, ranked 107th in the world, and were on a par with Polynesia ($824.7 million). The share in the world was 0.031%, and 0.14% in Asia.

The share of imports in GDP of Brunei was 18.9% in the 1980s, ranked 153rd in the world, and was on a par with Malawi (18.9%), Nicaragua (18.7%).

The Brunei's imports per capita were $3 664.7 in the 1980s, ranked 34th in the world, and were on a par with Canada ($3.7 thousand), French Polynesia ($3.7 thousand), Western Europe ($3.8 thousand). The imports per capita in Brunei were greater than imports per capita in the world ($539.1) in 6.8 times, and were greater than imports per capita in Asia ($211.9) in 17.3 times.

The growth of imports in Brunei was 4.1% in the 1980s, ranked 66th in the world, and was on a par with São Tomé and Príncipe (4.1%), Europe (4.1%). The growth of imports in Brunei (4.1%) was greater than growth of imports in the world (3.8%), was less than growth of imports in Asia (4.9%).

Comparison with neighbors. The imports of Brunei were less than in Malaysia ($16.9 billion). The value of imports per capita in Brunei was greater than in Malaysia ($1 092.1). The growth of imports in Brunei was less than in Malaysia (9.2%).

Comparison with leaders. The Brunei's imports were less than in the United States ($417.2 billion), in Germany ($225.6 billion), in Japan ($175.9 billion), in France ($162.0 billion), and in the United Kingdom ($157.7 billion). The Brunei's imports per capita were greater than in Germany ($2.9 thousand), in France ($2.9 thousand), in the UK ($2.8 thousand), in the United States ($1 742.4), and in Japan ($1 450.4). The growth of imports in Brunei was greater than in Germany (3.3%); but less than in the USA (5.8%), in the United Kingdom (5.1%), in Japan (4.6%), and in France (4.3%).

The 1990s

The Brunei's imports were $2.1 billion per year in the 1990s, ranked 114th in the world, and were on a par with Yemen ($2.1 billion), Kosovo ($2.1 billion). The share in the world was 0.036%, and 0.14% in Asia.

The share of imports in GDP of Brunei was 43.7% in the 1990s, ranked 85th in the world, and was on a par with Thailand (43.7%), Costa Rica (43.7%), Mongolia (43.6%).

The value of imports per capita in Brunei was $7 158.4 in the 1990s, ranked 30th in the world, and was on a par with Kuwait ($7.2 thousand), the TCI ($7.1 thousand). The imports per capita in Brunei were greater than imports per capita in the world ($1 015.5) in 7.0 times, and were greater than imports per capita in Asia ($430.1) in 16.6 times.

The growth of imports in Brunei was 4.6% in the 1990s, ranked 100th in the world, and was on a par with Sweden (4.6%), Palau (4.6%), the Cayman Islands (4.6%). The growth of imports in Brunei (4.6%) was less than growth of imports in the world (6.6%), was less than growth of imports in Asia (6.8%).

Comparison with neighbors. The value of imports in Brunei was less than in Malaysia ($65.1 billion). The Brunei's imports per capita were greater than in Malaysia ($3.2 thousand). The growth of imports in Brunei was less than in Malaysia (11.6%).

Comparison with leaders. The Brunei's imports were less than in the United States ($874.1 billion), in Germany ($501.6 billion), in Japan ($355.9 billion), in the United Kingdom ($330.2 billion), and in France ($308.5 billion). The value of imports per capita in Brunei was greater than in Germany ($6.2 thousand), in the UK ($5.7 thousand), in France ($5.2 thousand), in the USA ($3.3 thousand), and in Japan ($2.8 thousand). The growth of imports in Brunei was greater than in Japan (3.3%); but less than in the United States (8.3%), in Germany (6.4%), in France (5.1%), and in the UK (5.1%).

The 2000s

The imports of Brunei were $2.7 billion per year in the 2000s, ranked 132nd in the world, and were on a par with Nepal ($2.7 billion), Chad ($2.6 billion). The share in the world was 0.022%, and 0.075% in Asia.

The structure of imports: primary products (9.6%), resource-based manufactures (14.5%), low technology manufactures (21.6%), medium technology manufactures (38.1%), and high technology manufactures (14.2%).

Brunei imported goods from Singapore (29.6%), Malaysia (18.4%), the UK (15.2%), Japan (7.0%), the United States (4.5%) and other countries (25.3%).

The share of imports in GDP of Brunei was 26.7% in the 2000s, ranked 178th in the world, and was on a par with Uruguay (27.0%), the World (26.5%), France (27.0%).

The value of imports per capita in Brunei was $7 413.3 in the 2000s, ranked 51st in the world, and was on a par with Palau ($7.4 thousand), Czechia ($7.5 thousand), Spain ($7.3 thousand). The Brunei's imports per capita were greater than imports per capita in the world ($1 899.9) in 3.9 times, and were greater than imports per capita in Asia ($898.2) in 8.3 times.

The growth of imports in Brunei was 3.4% in the 2000s, ranked 136th in the world, and was on a par with the Comoros (3.4%), Togo (3.4%), Greece (3.4%). The growth of imports in Brunei (3.4%) was less than growth of imports in the world (5.1%), was less than growth of imports in Asia (7.8%).

Comparison with neighbors. The Brunei's imports were less than in Malaysia ($125.4 billion). The Brunei's imports per capita were greater than in Malaysia ($4.9 thousand). The growth of imports in Brunei was less than in Malaysia (5.4%).

Comparison with leaders. The value of imports in Brunei was less than in the USA ($1.9 trillion), in Germany ($914.7 billion), in United Kingdom ($641.8 billion), in China ($641.1 billion), and in Japan ($566.4 billion). The value of imports per capita in Brunei was greater than in the USA ($6.4 thousand), in Japan ($4.4 thousand), and in China ($483.3); but less than in Germany ($11.2 thousand) and in the UK ($10.6 thousand). The growth of imports in Brunei was greater than in the United Kingdom (3.1%), in the USA (2.8%), and in Japan (1.8%); but less than in China (15.1%) and in Germany (3.7%).

The 2010s

The Brunei's imports were $5.6 billion per year in the 2010s, ranked 134th in the world, and were on a par with Kyrgyzstan ($5.5

billion), Moldova ($5.5 billion). The share in the world was 0.025%, and 0.070% in Asia.

The structure of imports: primary products (9.9%), resource-based manufactures (20.5%), low technology manufactures (16.1%), medium technology manufactures (39.5%), and high technology manufactures (12.5%).

Brunei imported goods from Singapore (23.9%), China (22.9%), Malaysia (13.0%), the United Kingdom (10.2%), the USA (6.2%) and other countries (23.8%).

The share of imports in GDP of Brunei was 37.2% in the 2010s, ranked 131st in the world, and was on a par with Central America (37.1%), Eastern Europe (37.3%), Zimbabwe (37.3%).

The imports per capita in Brunei were $13 546.2 in the 2010s, ranked 42nd in the world, and were on a par with Kuwait ($13.7 thousand). The Brunei's imports per capita were greater than imports per capita in the world ($3 015.6) in 4.5 times, and were greater than imports per capita in Asia ($1 813.7) in 7.5 times.

The growth of imports in Brunei was 5.5% in the 2010s, ranked 65th in the world, and was on a par with Iceland (5.5%). The growth of imports in Brunei (5.5%) was greater than growth of imports in the world (4.4%), was greater than growth of imports in Asia (5.4%).

Comparison with neighbors. The value of imports in Brunei was 36.6 times lower than in Malaysia ($204.1 billion). The value of imports per capita in Brunei was 99.6% higher than in Malaysia ($6.8 thousand). The growth of imports in Brunei was greater than in Malaysia (4.1%).

Comparison with leaders. The imports of Brunei were 505.2 times lower than in the USA ($2.8 trillion), 371.0 times lower than in China ($2.1 trillion), 260.8 times lower than in Germany ($1.5 trillion), 157.4 times lower than in Japan ($877.9 billion), and 153.3 times lower than in the UK ($854.8 billion). The imports per capita in Brunei were 4.0% higher than in the United Kingdom ($13.0 thousand), 53.6% higher than in the United States ($8.8 thousand), 97.4% higher than in Japan ($6.9 thousand), and 9.2 times higher than in China ($1 475.4); but 23.8% lower than in Germany ($17.8 thousand). The growth of imports in Brunei was greater than in Germany (4.8%), in the USA (4.4%), in Japan (3.8%), and in the UK (3.6%); but less than in China (8.2%).

Part IV. Consumption

Chapter XII. Government consumption expenditure

General government final consumption expenditure

The government consumption expenditure of Brunei increased from $142.3 million per year in the 1970s to $3.3 billion per year in the 2010s, that is by $3.2 billion or 23.5 times. The change occurred at $2.6 billion due to a 4.4-fold increase in prices, as also at $388.7 million due to a 2.1-fold increase in per capita rate, as well as at $227.4 million due to the rise in population. The average annual growth in government consumption expenditure is 4.7%. The minimum value of public expenditure was in 1970 at $20.6 million. The maximum value of government consumption expenditure was in 2014 at $3.7 billion.

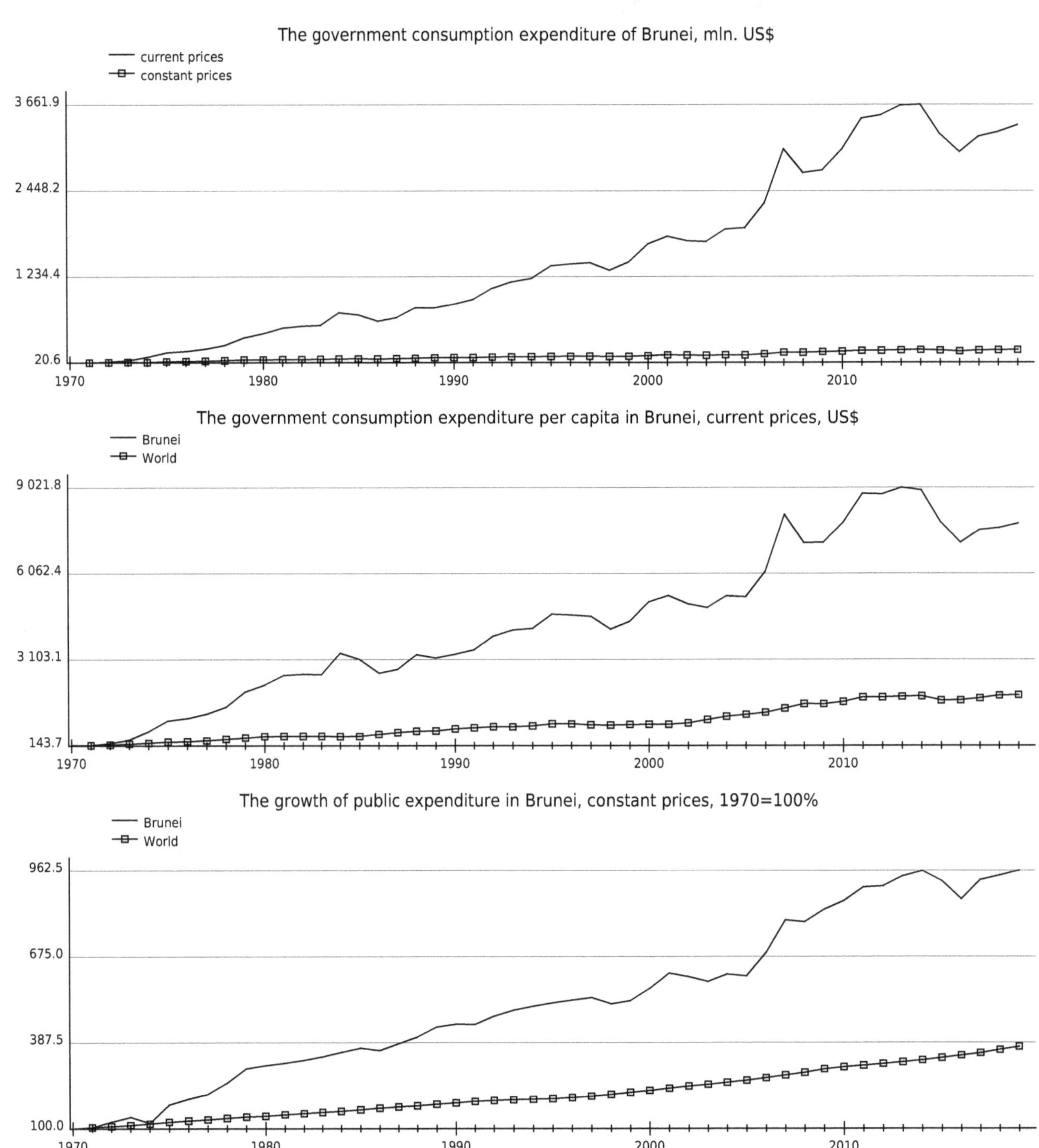

The government consumption expenditure of Brunei, mln. US$

The government consumption expenditure per capita in Brunei, current prices, US$

The growth of public expenditure in Brunei, constant prices, 1970=100%

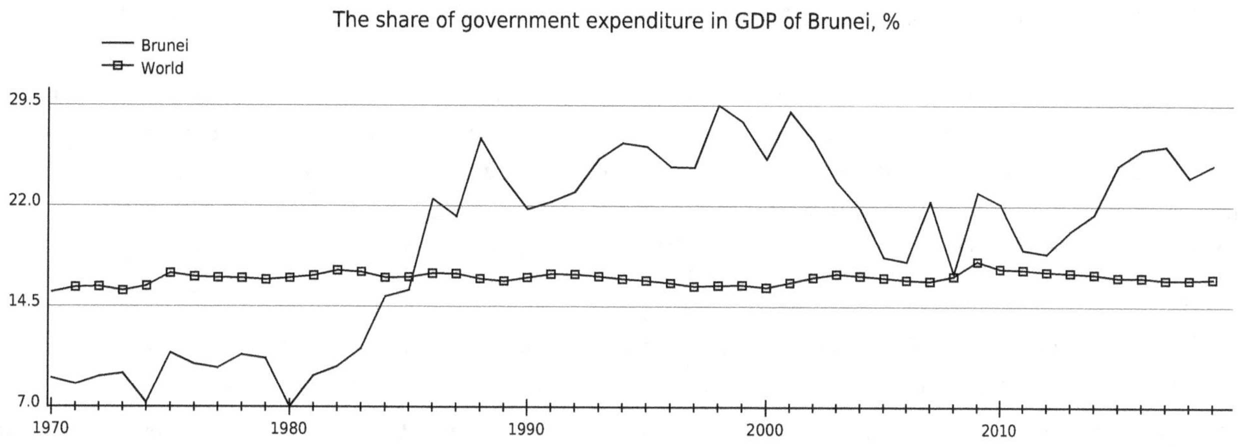

The 1970s

The Brunei's public expenditure was $142.3 million per year in the 1970s, ranked 111th in the world, and was on a par with New Caledonia ($142.1 million), Paraguay ($142.8 million), Suriname ($140.4 million). The share in the world was 0.013%, and 0.089% in Asia.

The share of public expenditure in GDP of Brunei was 10.1% in the 1970s, ranked 149th in the world, and was on a par with the Cayman Islands (10.1%), Republic of Korea (10.2%).

The Brunei's government expenditure per capita was $898.0 in the 1970s, ranked 28th in the world, and was on a par with Oceania ($920.9). The Brunei's public expenditure per capita was greater than public expenditure per capita in the world ($265.2) in 3.4 times, and was greater than government consumption expenditure per capita in Asia ($68.9) in 13.0 times.

The growth of government expenditure in Brunei was 13% in the 1970s, ranked 10th in the world. The growth of government consumption expenditure in Brunei (13.0%) was greater than growth of government consumption expenditure in the world (3.7%), was greater than growth of government consumption expenditure in Asia (6.9%).

Comparison with neighbors. The Brunei's government consumption expenditure was less than in Malaysia ($1.6 billion). The government expenditure per capita in Brunei was greater than in Malaysia ($134.0). The growth of public expenditure in Brunei was greater than in Malaysia (9.7%).

Comparison with leaders. The Brunei's government expenditure was less than in the United States ($285.9 billion), in the USSR ($117.3 billion), in Germany ($95.6 billion), in Japan ($78.0 billion), and in France ($64.5 billion). The government expenditure per capita in Brunei was greater than in Japan ($700.2) and in the USSR ($465.0); but less than in the USA ($1 310.2), in Germany ($1 213.7), and in France ($1 202.3). The growth of government consumption expenditure in Brunei was greater than in the USSR (7.2%), in Japan (5.3%), in France (5.0%), in Germany (4.4%), and in the USA (0.94%).

The 1980s

The Brunei's government expenditure was $630.4 million per year in the 1980s, ranked 94th in the world, and was on a par with Honduras ($625.7 million), Yemen ($638.7 million), Costa Rica ($645.9 million). The share in the world was 0.025%, and 0.13% in Asia.

The share of government expenditure in GDP of Brunei was 14.6% in the 1980s, ranked 119th in the world, and was on a par with Puerto Rico (14.6%), Kenya (14.7%), Honduras (14.5%).

The Brunei's government consumption expenditure per capita was $2 841.0 in the 1980s, ranked 15th in the world, and was on a par with France ($2.8 thousand), Northern America ($2.8 thousand), Finland ($2.8 thousand). The Brunei's public expenditure per capita was greater than public expenditure per capita in the world ($523.5) in 5.4 times, and was greater than public expenditure per capita in Asia ($170.1) in 16.7 times.

The growth of government consumption expenditure in Brunei was 3.8% in the 1980s, ranked 79th in the world, and was on a par with Cuba (3.8%). The growth of government expenditure in Brunei (3.8%) was greater than growth of government expenditure in the world (2.7%), was less than growth of public expenditure in Asia (4.2%).

Comparison with neighbors. The Brunei's government consumption expenditure was less than in Malaysia ($4.8 billion). The Brunei's public expenditure per capita was greater than in Malaysia ($309.3). The growth of public expenditure in Brunei was less than in Malaysia (5.8%).

Comparison with leaders. The Brunei's government consumption expenditure was less than in the United States ($665.3 billion), in Japan ($257.4 billion), in Germany ($203.7 billion), in the USSR ($181.1 billion), and in France ($159.8 billion). The government consumption expenditure per capita in Brunei was greater than in France ($2.8 thousand), in the United States ($2.8 thousand), in Germany ($2.6 thousand), in Japan ($2.1 thousand), and in the USSR ($658.0). The growth of government expenditure in Brunei was greater than in Japan (3.5%), in France (2.8%), in the USA (2.6%), and in Germany (0.98%); but less than in the USSR (5.4%).

The 1990s

The public expenditure of Brunei was $1.2 billion per year in the 1990s, ranked 90th in the world, and was on a par with Cyprus ($1.2 billion), Botswana ($1.2 billion), Polynesia ($1.2 billion). The share in the world was 0.026%, and 0.11% in Asia.

The share of public expenditure in GDP of Brunei was 25.4% in the 1990s, ranked 31st in the world, and was on a par with Samoa (25.4%), Vanuatu (25.4%).

The Brunei's government expenditure per capita was $4 166.0 in the 1990s, ranked 27th in the world. The Brunei's government expenditure per capita was greater than government expenditure per capita in the world ($824.8) in 5.1 times, and was greater than government expenditure per capita in Asia ($318.7) in 13.1 times.

The growth of government consumption expenditure in Brunei was 1.8% in the 1990s, ranked 118th in the world. The growth of public expenditure in Brunei (1.8%) was less than growth of government consumption expenditure in the world (2.0%), was less than growth of government expenditure in Asia (5.0%).

Comparison with neighbors. The Brunei's public expenditure was less than in Malaysia ($8.7 billion). The Brunei's government consumption expenditure per capita was greater than in Malaysia ($427.9). The growth of government consumption expenditure in Brunei was less than in Malaysia (5.7%).

Comparison with leaders. The government consumption expenditure of Brunei was less than in the USA ($1.1 trillion), in Japan ($651.8 billion), in Germany ($419.6 billion), in France ($325.4 billion), and in the United Kingdom ($234.6 billion). The Brunei's government consumption expenditure per capita was greater than in the UK ($4.1 thousand); but less than in France ($5.5 thousand), in Germany ($5.2 thousand), in Japan ($5.2 thousand), and in the United States ($4.3 thousand). The growth of government expenditure in Brunei was greater than in France (1.8%) and in the United States (1.3%); but less than in Japan (3.0%), in Germany (2.4%), and in the UK (2.1%).

The 2000s

The Brunei's government expenditure was $2.2 billion per year in the 2000s, ranked 96th in the world, and was on a par with Bahrain ($2.2 billion), Panama ($2.2 billion), Tanzania ($2.1 billion). The share in the world was 0.028%, and 0.11% in Asia.

The share of government expenditure in GDP of Brunei was 21.5% in the 2000s, ranked 35th in the world, and was on a par with Finland (21.4%).

The government expenditure per capita in Brunei was $5 970.1 in the 2000s, ranked 29th in the world, and was on a par with Australasia ($5.9 thousand), Italy ($5.8 thousand). The Brunei's government consumption expenditure per capita was greater than government consumption expenditure per capita in the world ($1 200.9) in 5.0 times, and was greater than public expenditure per capita in Asia ($477.4) in 12.5 times.

The growth of government consumption expenditure in Brunei was 4.7% in the 2000s, ranked 77th in the world, and was on a par with South Africa (4.6%), Macao (4.6%). The growth of government consumption expenditure in Brunei (4.7%) was greater than growth of public expenditure in the world (3.1%), was less than growth of government expenditure in Asia (5.3%).

Comparison with neighbors. The government consumption expenditure of Brunei was less than in Malaysia ($17.4 billion). The government expenditure per capita in Brunei was greater than in Malaysia ($682.4). The growth of public expenditure in Brunei was less than in Malaysia (7.5%).

Comparison with leaders. The government consumption expenditure of Brunei was less than in the United States ($1.9 trillion), in Japan ($844.2 billion), in Germany ($520.1 billion), in France ($479.9 billion), and in the United Kingdom ($453.4 billion). The Brunei's public expenditure per capita was less than in France ($7.6 thousand), in the UK ($7.5 thousand), in Japan ($6.6 thousand), in the USA ($6.5 thousand), and in Germany ($6.4 thousand). The growth of public expenditure in Brunei was greater than in the UK (2.9%), in the USA (2.2%), in Japan (1.7%), in France (1.7%), and in Germany (1.4%).

The 2010s

The Brunei's government expenditure was $3.3 billion per year in the 2010s, ranked 111th in the world, and was on a par with Turkmenistan ($3.3 billion), Mozambique ($3.4 billion), Trinidad and Tobago ($3.3 billion). The share in the world was 0.026%, and 0.078% in Asia.

The share of government consumption expenditure in GDP of Brunei was 22.3% in the 2010s, ranked 36th in the world, and was on a par with the Seychelles (22.3%), Norway (22.4%).

The Brunei's government expenditure per capita was $8 117.2 in the 2010s, ranked 27th in the world, and was on a par with Japan ($8.2 thousand), the USA ($8.3 thousand). The public expenditure per capita in Brunei was greater than public expenditure per capita in the world ($1 785.1) in 4.5 times, and was greater than public expenditure per capita in Asia ($970.7) in 8.4 times.

The growth of public expenditure in Brunei was 1.5% in the 2010s, ranked 131st in the world. The growth of public expenditure in Brunei (1.5%) was less than growth of government consumption expenditure in the world (2.3%), was less than growth of public expenditure in Asia (5.2%).

Comparison with neighbors. The government consumption expenditure of Brunei was 12.2 times lower than in Malaysia ($40.6 billion). The government consumption expenditure per capita in Brunei was 6.0 times higher than in Malaysia ($1 350.6). The growth of public expenditure in Brunei was less than in Malaysia (4.9%).

Comparison with leaders. The public expenditure of Brunei was 794.0 times lower than in the USA ($2.7 trillion), 502.4 times lower than in China ($1.7 trillion), 312.1 times lower than in Japan ($1.0 trillion), 215.9 times lower than in Germany ($721.6 billion), and 190.9 times lower than in France ($637.9 billion). The government consumption expenditure per capita in Brunei was 6.8 times higher than in China ($1 197.3); but 15.6% lower than in France ($9.6 thousand), 7.9% lower than in Germany ($8.8 thousand), 2.3% lower than in the United States ($8.3 thousand), and 0.44% lower than in Japan ($8.2 thousand). The growth of government consumption expenditure in Brunei was greater than in Japan (1.3%), in France (1.3%), and in the USA (0.0052%); but less than in China (8.3%) and in Germany (1.9%).

Chapter XIII. Household consumption expenditure

(including Non-profit institutions serving households)

The Brunei's household expenditure rose from $126.6 million per year in the 1970s to $2.5 billion per year in the 2010s, that is by $2.4 billion or 20.0 times. The change occurred at $2.3 billion due to a 10.5-fold increase in prices, as also at -$89.3 million due to a 1.4-fold decrease in per capita rate, as well as at $202.3 million due to the growing in population. The average annual growth in household consumption expenditure is 1.8%. The minimum value of household consumption expenditure was in 1970 at $35.3 million. The maximum value of household expenditure was in 2013 at $2.8 billion.

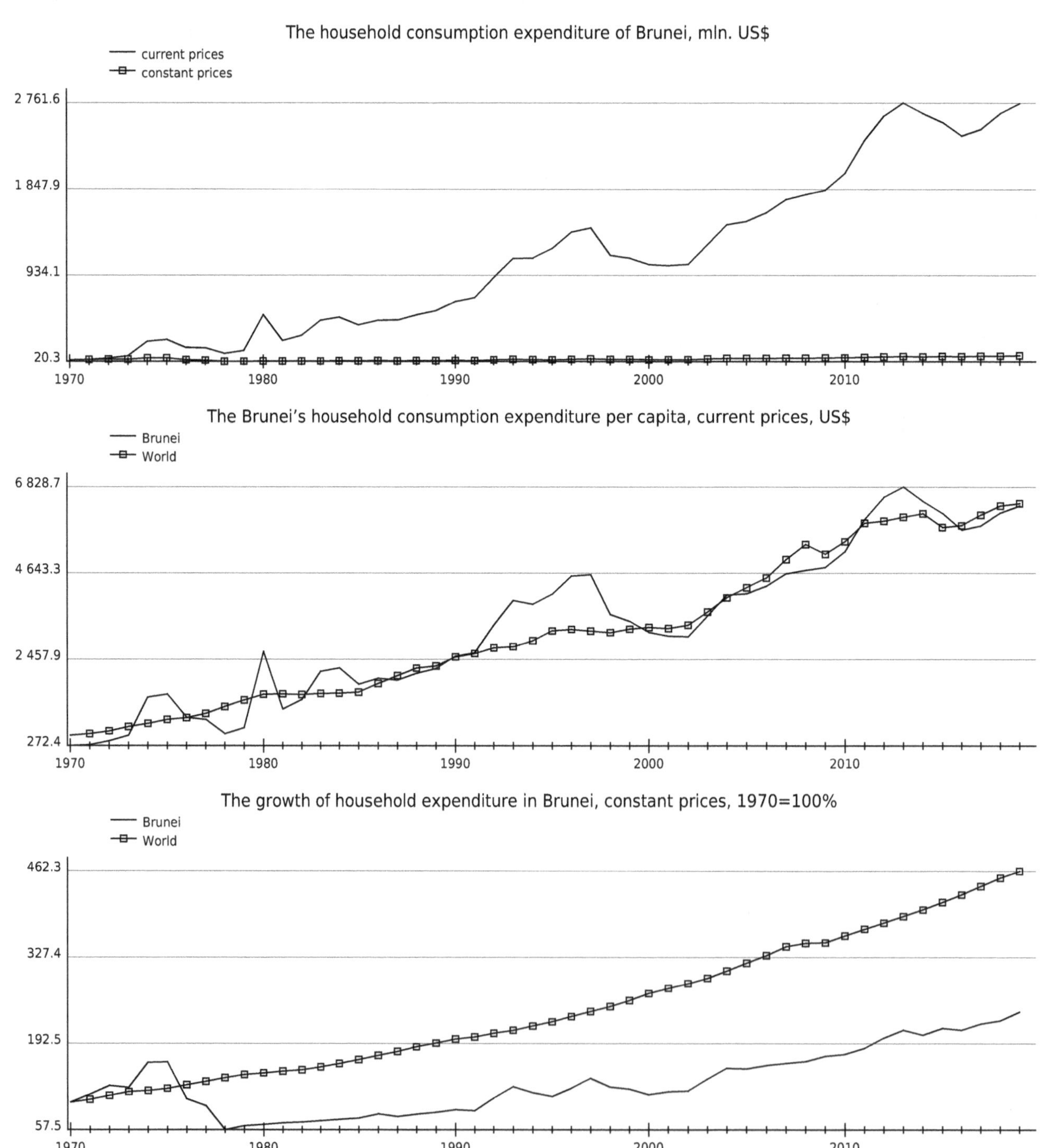

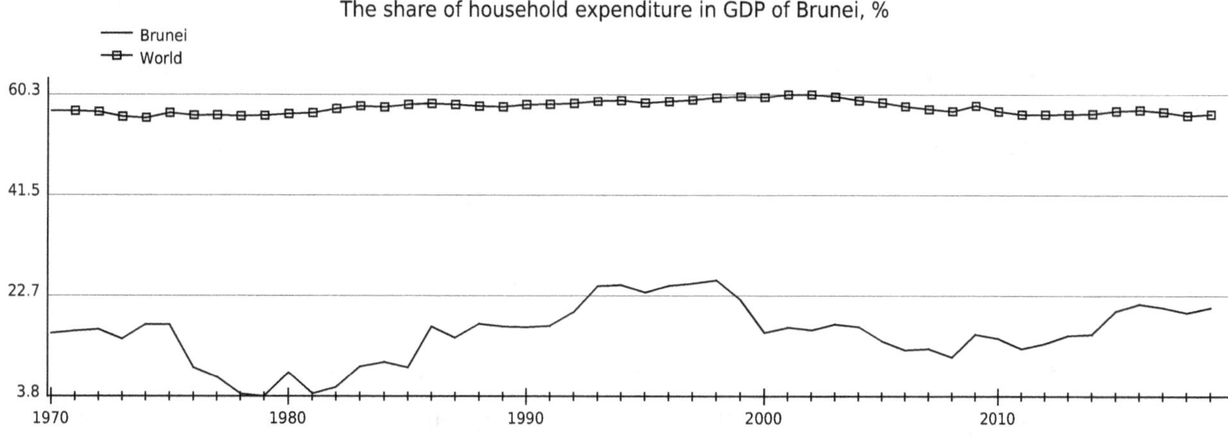

The 1970s

The household expenditure of Brunei was $126.6 million per year in the 1970s, ranked 152nd in the world. The share in the world was 0.0034%, and 0.019% in Asia.

The share of household expenditure in GDP of Brunei was 9.0% in the 1970s, ranked 184th in the world, and was on a par with Nigeria (9.0%).

The household expenditure per capita in Brunei was $798.9 in the 1970s, ranked 72nd in the world, and was on a par with the Caribbean ($811.8), Bulgaria ($813.5). The household expenditure per capita in Brunei was less than household expenditure per capita in the world ($914.8) by 12.7%, and was greater than household consumption expenditure per capita in Asia ($282.4) in 2.8 times.

The growth of household consumption expenditure in Brunei was -4.9% in the 1970s, ranked 183rd in the world. The growth of household consumption expenditure in Brunei (-4.9%) was less than growth of household consumption expenditure in the world (4.1%), was less than growth of household expenditure in Asia (5.2%).

Comparison with neighbors. The household consumption expenditure of Brunei was less than in Malaysia ($5.4 billion). The Brunei's household consumption expenditure per capita was greater than in Malaysia ($449.9). The growth of household expenditure in Brunei was less than in Malaysia (9.0%).

Comparison with leaders. The Brunei's household expenditure was less than in the USA ($1.0 trillion), in the USSR ($310.6 billion), in Japan ($280.9 billion), in Germany ($277.8 billion), and in France ($180.7 billion). The Brunei's household expenditure per capita was less than in the United States ($4.7 thousand), in Germany ($3.5 thousand), in France ($3.4 thousand), in Japan ($2.5 thousand), and in the USSR ($1 231.6). The growth of household consumption expenditure in Brunei was less than in Japan (5.1%), in the USSR (4.7%), in France (4.0%), in the United States (3.6%), and in Germany (3.6%).

The 1980s

The household consumption expenditure of Brunei was $439.4 million per year in the 1980s, ranked 148th in the world. The share in the world was 0.0050%, and 0.023% in Asia.

The share of household consumption expenditure in GDP of Brunei was 10.2% in the 1980s, ranked 184th in the world.

The household consumption expenditure per capita in Brunei was $1 980.2 in the 1980s, ranked 58th in the world, and was on a par with Oman ($1 973.8), the British Virgin Islands ($1 968.1), Saint Lucia ($2.0 thousand). The Brunei's household consumption expenditure per capita was greater than household consumption expenditure per capita in the world ($1 808.0) by 9.5%, and was greater than household expenditure per capita in Asia ($666.0) in 3.0 times.

The growth of household expenditure in Brunei was 2.9% in the 1980s, ranked 93rd in the world, and was on a par with the Americas (2.9%), the Philippines (2.9%). The growth of household expenditure in Brunei (2.9%) was less than growth of household expenditure in the world (3.0%), was less than growth of household consumption expenditure in Asia (4.7%).

Comparison with neighbors. The household expenditure of Brunei was less than in Malaysia ($15.5 billion). The Brunei's household expenditure per capita was greater than in Malaysia ($1 000.0). The growth of household consumption expenditure in Brunei was less than in Malaysia (4.9%).

Comparison with leaders. The Brunei's household expenditure was less than in the USA ($2.6 trillion), in Japan ($945.6 billion), in Germany ($575.7 billion), in the USSR ($424.6 billion), and in the United Kingdom ($416.5 billion). The Brunei's household consumption expenditure per capita was greater than in the USSR ($1 542.8); but less than in the USA ($10.9 thousand), in Japan ($7.8 thousand), in Germany ($7.4 thousand), and in the UK ($7.4 thousand). The growth of household consumption expenditure in Brunei was greater than in Germany (1.8%); but less than in Japan (3.7%), in the UK (3.5%), in the United States (3.2%), and in the USSR (3.0%).

The 1990s

The household consumption expenditure of Brunei was $1.1 billion per year in the 1990s, ranked 158th in the world. The share in the world was 0.0064%, and 0.026% in Asia.

The share of household expenditure in GDP of Brunei was 22.5% in the 1990s, ranked 207th in the world.

The Brunei's household expenditure per capita was $3 689.7 in the 1990s, ranked 59th in the world, and was on a par with Saint Lucia ($3.7 thousand). The Brunei's household expenditure per capita was greater than household expenditure per capita in the world ($2 963.9) by 24.5%, and was greater than household consumption expenditure per capita in Asia ($1 208.2) in 3.1 times.

The growth of household consumption expenditure in Brunei was 3.6% in the 1990s, ranked 75th in the world, and was on a par with Bolivia (3.6%), South America (3.6%), Jamaica (3.6%). The growth of household consumption expenditure in Brunei (3.6%) was greater than growth of household consumption expenditure in the world (3.0%), was less than growth of household expenditure in Asia (4.4%).

Comparison with neighbors. The household consumption expenditure of Brunei was less than in Malaysia ($34.4 billion). The household expenditure per capita in Brunei was greater than in Malaysia ($1 694.1). The growth of household expenditure in Brunei was less than in Malaysia (5.5%).

Comparison with leaders. The household expenditure of Brunei was less than in the United States ($4.9 trillion), in Japan ($2.3 trillion), in Germany ($1.2 trillion), in the UK ($884.5 billion), and in France ($783.0 billion). The Brunei's household consumption expenditure per capita was less than in the United States ($18.5 thousand), in Japan ($18.2 thousand), in the UK ($15.3 thousand), in Germany ($15.2 thousand), and in France ($13.2 thousand). The growth of household consumption expenditure in Brunei was greater than in the United States (3.4%), in the UK (2.8%), in Germany (2.1%), in Japan (1.8%), and in France (1.8%).

The 2000s

The household expenditure of Brunei was $1.4 billion per year in the 2000s, ranked 166th in the world. The share in the world was 0.0052%, and 0.022% in Asia.

The share of household consumption expenditure in GDP of Brunei was 14.3% in the 2000s, ranked 209th in the world.

The Brunei's household expenditure per capita was $3 977.2 in the 2000s, ranked 80th in the world, and was on a par with the Cook Islands ($4.1 thousand), Saudi Arabia ($4.1 thousand). The Brunei's household consumption expenditure per capita was less than household consumption expenditure per capita in the world ($4 208.2) by 5.5%, and was greater than household expenditure per capita in Asia ($1 649.6) in 2.4 times.

The growth of household expenditure in Brunei was 3.6% in the 2000s, ranked 118th in the world, and was on a par with Kiribati (3.6%), Malawi (3.6%), Niger (3.6%). The growth of household consumption expenditure in Brunei (3.6%) was greater than growth of household expenditure in the world (3.0%), was less than growth of household consumption expenditure in Asia (4.4%).

Comparison with neighbors. The household expenditure of Brunei was less than in Malaysia ($65.8 billion). The Brunei's household consumption expenditure per capita was greater than in Malaysia ($2.6 thousand). The growth of household consumption expenditure in Brunei was less than in Malaysia (7.3%).

Comparison with leaders. The Brunei's household consumption expenditure was less than in the United States ($8.5 trillion), in Japan ($2.6 trillion), in Germany ($1.5 trillion), in the United Kingdom ($1.5 trillion), and in France ($1.1 trillion). The Brunei's household consumption expenditure per capita was less than in the USA ($28.8 thousand), in the United Kingdom ($25.0 thousand), in Japan ($20.4 thousand), in Germany ($18.9 thousand), and in France ($18.1 thousand). The growth of household consumption expenditure in Brunei was greater than in the USA (2.4%), in the United Kingdom (2.1%), in France (2.0%), in Japan (0.81%), and in Germany (0.46%).

The 2010s

The household expenditure of Brunei was $2.5 billion per year in the 2010s, ranked 165th in the world. The share in the world was 0.0057%, and 0.019% in Asia.

The share of household expenditure in GDP of Brunei was 16.9% in the 2010s, ranked 209th in the world.

The Brunei's household consumption expenditure per capita was $6 139.3 in the 2010s, ranked 86th in the world, and was on a par with Romania ($6.2 thousand), Oman ($6.2 thousand), the World ($6.0 thousand). The household expenditure per capita in Brunei was greater than household consumption expenditure per capita in the world ($6 018.5) by 2.0%, and was greater than household expenditure per capita in Asia ($2 977.2) in 2.1 times.

The growth of household expenditure in Brunei was 3.4% in the 2010s, ranked 92nd in the world, and was on a par with Estonia (3.4%). The growth of household consumption expenditure in Brunei (3.4%) was greater than growth of household expenditure in the world (2.8%), was less than growth of household expenditure in Asia (4.9%).

Comparison with neighbors. The Brunei's household expenditure was 67.1 times lower than in Malaysia ($169.5 billion). The Brunei's household consumption expenditure per capita was 8.9% higher than in Malaysia ($5.6 thousand). The growth of household consumption expenditure in Brunei was less than in Malaysia (7.1%).

Comparison with leaders. The household expenditure of Brunei was 4 823.7 times lower than in the United States ($12.2 trillion), 1 554.7 times lower than in China ($3.9 trillion), 1 181.9 times lower than in Japan ($3.0 trillion), 774.8 times lower than in Germany ($2.0 trillion), and 705.0 times lower than in the United Kingdom ($1.8 trillion). The Brunei's household expenditure per capita was 2.2 times higher than in China ($2.8 thousand); but 6.2 times lower than in the United States ($38.2 thousand), 4.4 times lower than in the United Kingdom ($27.2 thousand), 3.9 times lower than in Germany ($23.9 thousand), and 3.8 times lower than in Japan ($23.4 thousand). The growth of household consumption expenditure in Brunei was greater than in the United States (2.4%), in the United Kingdom (1.8%), in Germany (1.4%), and in Japan (0.64%); but less than in China (8.3%).

Chapter XIV. Food consumption

During the research period the food consumption grew in treenuts (in 4.2 times), stimulants (in 4.1 times), meat (in 2.2 times), milk (in 2.0 times), vegetable oils (by 88.8%), eggs (by 38.6%), fruits (by 35.3%), fish (by 33.3%), cereals (by 22.4%), vegetables (by 19.9%), sugar (by 17.7%), but fell in spices (by 2.6%), starchy roots (by 26.8%), alcoholic beverages (by 36.6%), pulses (by 95.5%).

These are the correlation coefficients between the GNI per capita in constant prices and the food consumption: vegetable oils (0.987), eggs (0.972), meat (0.95), stimulants (0.949), treenuts (0.924), fruits (0.806), milk (0.745), sugar (0.563), fish (0.56), vegetables (0.535), cereals (0.519), spices (0.121), starchy roots (-0.272), alcoholic beverages (-0.455), pulses (-0.835).

The 1970s

Kcal supply in Brunei was 2 177.8 kcal/capita/day in the 1970s, ranked 95th in the world, and was on a par with Sierra Leone (2 177.8 kcal/capita/day), Senegal (2 177.5 kcal/capita/day), Grenada (2 176.2 kcal/capita/day). Kcal supply in Brunei was less than in the world (2 403.2 kcal/capita/day), and was greater than in Asia (2 080.9 kcal/capita/day). Structure of kcal supply: cereals (45.8%), sugar (18.3%), meat (6.4%), vegetable oils (6.2%), starchy roots (3.2%), and others (20.1%).

Protein supply in Brunei was 56.9 g/capita/day in the 1970s, ranked 92nd in the world, and was on a par with Fiji (56.4 g/capita/day), the Caribbean (57.4 g/capita/day). Protein supply in Brunei was less than in the world (65.0 g/capita/day), and was greater than in Asia (52.3 g/capita/day). Structure of protein supply: cereals (35.7%), meat (22.2%), fish (13.2%), eggs (6.3%), milk (5.3%), and others (17.3%).

Fat supply in Brunei was 45.2 g/capita/day in the 1970s, ranked 93rd in the world, and was on a par with Senegal (45.3 g/capita/day), Bolivia (45.2 g/capita/day). Fat supply in Brunei was less than in the world (55.1 g/capita/day), and was greater than in Asia (31.8 g/capita/day). Structure of fat supply: vegetable oils (33.9%), meat (21%), milk (7.6%), eggs (7%), cereals (6.4%), and others (24.1%).

These are the levels of food consumption in the world rankings: 4th - spices (2.7 kg/capita/yr), 22nd - eggs (11.3 kg/capita/yr), 23rd - fish (30.3 kg/capita/yr), 32nd - sugar (42.2 kg/capita/yr), 48th - meat (37.5 kg/capita/yr), 51st - treenuts (0.80 kg/capita/yr), 54th - vegetables (54.6 kg/capita/yr), 61st - stimulants (2.2 kg/capita/yr), 71st - fruits (60.3 kg/capita/yr), 87th - vegetable oils (5.6 kg/capita/yr), 88th - cereals (109.0 kg/capita/yr), 93rd - alcoholic beverages (14.7 kg/capita/yr), 95th - starchy roots (29.0 kg/capita/yr), 99th - milk (34.7 kg/capita/yr), 111th - pulses (2.3 kg/capita/yr).

The 1980s

Kcal supply in Brunei was 2 687.3 kcal/capita/day in the 1980s, ranked 58th in the world, and was on a par with Micronesia (2 689.8 kcal/capita/day), Kiribati (2 689.8 kcal/capita/day), Mauritius (2 690.5 kcal/capita/day). Kcal supply in Brunei was greater than in the world (2 572.3 kcal/capita/day), and was greater than in Asia (2 333.4 kcal/capita/day). Structure of kcal supply: cereals (45.3%), sugar (13.8%), meat (9%), vegetable oils (5.8%), milk (5.8%), and others (20.3%).

Protein supply in Brunei was 80.1 g/capita/day in the 1980s, ranked 45th in the world, and was on a par with Lebanon (80.2 g/capita/day), Macao (79.8 g/capita/day), the Bahamas (79.5 g/capita/day). Protein supply in Brunei was greater than in the world (69.1 g/capita/day), and was greater than in Asia (58.8 g/capita/day). Structure of protein supply: cereals (33%), meat (24.8%), fish (12.2%), milk (8%), eggs (4.7%), and others (17.3%).

Fat supply in Brunei was 65.8 g/capita/day in the 1980s, ranked 69th in the world, and was on a par with South Africa (66.1 g/capita/day), Jordan (65.3 g/capita/day). Fat supply in Brunei was greater than in the world (63.2 g/capita/day), and was greater than in Asia (42.6 g/capita/day). Structure of fat supply: vegetable oils (26.9%), meat (26.2%), milk (10.5%), cereals (7.4%), eggs (5.2%), and others (23.8%).

These are the levels of food consumption in the world rankings: 2nd - spices (4.0 kg/capita/yr), 17th - fish (40.1 kg/capita/yr), 25th - eggs (12.0 kg/capita/yr), 29th - sugar (42.8 kg/capita/yr), 34th - treenuts (1.8 kg/capita/yr), 44th - meat (56.8 kg/capita/yr), 48th - stimulants (3.0 kg/capita/yr), 55th - cereals (140.0 kg/capita/yr), 57th - fruits (75.2 kg/capita/yr), 58th - vegetables (59.5 kg/capita/yr), 65th - alcoholic beverages (31.0 kg/capita/yr), 71st - milk (73.0 kg/capita/yr), 97th - vegetable oils (6.5 kg/capita/yr), 115th - pulses (2.4 kg/capita/yr), 121st - starchy roots (17.6 kg/capita/yr).

The 1990s

Kcal supply in Brunei was 2 826.2 kcal/capita/day in the 1990s, ranked 55th in the world, and was on a par with Malaysia (2 824.3

kcal/capita/day), South Africa (2 820.9 kcal/capita/day), Mauritius (2 832.9 kcal/capita/day). Kcal supply in Brunei was greater than in the world (2 652.6 kcal/capita/day), and was greater than in Asia (2 494.1 kcal/capita/day). Structure of kcal supply: cereals (48.1%), sugar (11.1%), meat (9.8%), vegetable oils (6.7%), milk (4.8%), and others (19.5%).

Protein supply in Brunei was 86.2 g/capita/day in the 1990s, ranked 47th in the world, and was on a par with the Americas (86.2 g/capita/day), Cyprus (86.0 g/capita/day), Tunisia (86.5 g/capita/day). Protein supply in Brunei was greater than in the world (72.1 g/capita/day), and was greater than in Asia (65.3 g/capita/day). Structure of protein supply: cereals (34%), meat (25.7%), fish (11.8%), milk (7.8%), eggs (5%), and others (15.7%).

Fat supply in Brunei was 74.7 g/capita/day in the 1990s, ranked 70th in the world, and was on a par with Costa Rica (75.1 g/capita/day), Chile (74.2 g/capita/day), Lithuania (74.0 g/capita/day). Fat supply in Brunei was greater than in the world (69.0 g/capita/day), and was greater than in Asia (54.3 g/capita/day). Structure of fat supply: vegetable oils (28.6%), meat (27.2%), milk (8.4%), cereals (7.5%), eggs (5.1%), and others (23.2%).

These are the levels of food consumption in the world rankings: 4th - spices (3.8 kg/capita/yr), 11th - eggs (13.7 kg/capita/yr), 17th - fish (38.4 kg/capita/yr), 27th - treenuts (2.9 kg/capita/yr), 33rd - stimulants (5.3 kg/capita/yr), 44th - meat (64.4 kg/capita/yr), 54th - sugar (37.9 kg/capita/yr), 56th - cereals (148.6 kg/capita/yr), 57th - vegetables (78.0 kg/capita/yr), 59th - fruits (84.7 kg/capita/yr), 95th - milk (72.2 kg/capita/yr), 99th - vegetable oils (7.8 kg/capita/yr), 128th - pulses (2.1 kg/capita/yr), 132nd - alcoholic beverages (6.6 kg/capita/yr), 144th - starchy roots (16.1 kg/capita/yr).

The 2000s

Kcal supply in Brunei was 2 923.3 kcal/capita/day in the 2000s, ranked 58th in the world, and was on a par with South Africa (2 922.9 kcal/capita/day), Central America (2 922.0 kcal/capita/day), Croatia (2 921.9 kcal/capita/day). Kcal supply in Brunei was greater than in the world (2 765.9 kcal/capita/day), and was greater than in Asia (2 619.0 kcal/capita/day). Structure of kcal supply: cereals (46%), sugar (12.1%), meat (9.2%), vegetable oils (8%), milk (5.3%), and others (19.4%).

Protein supply in Brunei was 87.0 g/capita/day in the 2000s, ranked 55th in the world, and was on a par with China (87.0 g/capita/day), Saint Lucia (87.0 g/capita/day), Latvia (87.1 g/capita/day). Protein supply in Brunei was greater than in the world (76.5 g/capita/day), and was greater than in Asia (70.9 g/capita/day). Structure of protein supply: cereals (32.5%), meat (26.4%), fish (10.8%), milk (9.7%), eggs (5.6%), and others (15%).

Fat supply in Brunei was 79.1 g/capita/day in the 2000s, ranked 85th in the world, and was on a par with South Africa (79.2 g/capita/day), the Dominican Republic (79.2 g/capita/day), Antigua and Barbuda (78.5 g/capita/day). Fat supply in Brunei was greater than in the world (76.9 g/capita/day), and was greater than in Asia (64.4 g/capita/day). Structure of fat supply: vegetable oils (33.6%), meat (23.8%), milk (7.8%), cereals (6.8%), eggs (5.4%), and others (22.6%).

These are the levels of food consumption in the world rankings: 3rd - spices (4.2 kg/capita/yr), 8th - eggs (15.4 kg/capita/yr), 21st - fish (35.3 kg/capita/yr), 33rd - treenuts (3.4 kg/capita/yr), 36th - stimulants (6.4 kg/capita/yr), 42nd - sugar (42.3 kg/capita/yr), 48th - meat (68.5 kg/capita/yr), 63rd - cereals (141.4 kg/capita/yr), 64th - fruits (90.2 kg/capita/yr), 84th - vegetables (73.5 kg/capita/yr), 89th - vegetable oils (9.8 kg/capita/yr), 90th - milk (91.3 kg/capita/yr), 133rd - pulses (1.9 kg/capita/yr), 146th - starchy roots (20.9 kg/capita/yr), 147th - alcoholic beverages (4.2 kg/capita/yr).

The 2010s

Kcal supply in Brunei was 2 947.5 kcal/capita/day in the 2010s, ranked 68th in the world, and was on a par with Trinidad and Tobago (2 947.0 kcal/capita/day), Chile (2 952.0 kcal/capita/day), Dominica (2 956.8 kcal/capita/day). Kcal supply in Brunei was greater than in the world (2 869.3 kcal/capita/day), and was greater than in Asia (2 759.8 kcal/capita/day). Structure of kcal supply: cereals (44.2%), sugar (13.1%), meat (10.5%), vegetable oils (8.7%), milk (4.6%), and others (18.9%).

Protein supply in Brunei was 89.2 g/capita/day in the 2010s, ranked 58th in the world, and was on a par with Western Asia (89.0 g/capita/day), Bermuda (89.4 g/capita/day), Czechia (89.5 g/capita/day). Protein supply in Brunei was greater than in the world (80.6 g/capita/day), and was greater than in Asia (76.7 g/capita/day). Structure of protein supply: meat (31.1%), cereals (30.1%), fish (11.4%), milk (7.3%), eggs (5.5%), and others (14.6%).

Fat supply in Brunei was 81.9 g/capita/day in the 2010s, ranked 87th in the world, and was on a par with the World (82.4 g/capita/day). Fat supply in Brunei was less than in the world (82.4 g/capita/day), and was greater than in Asia (72.1 g/capita/day). Structure of fat supply: vegetable oils (35.3%), meat (25.8%), milk (7%), cereals (6.2%), eggs (5.4%), and others (20.3%).

These are the levels of food consumption in the world rankings: 7th - eggs (15.7 kg/capita/yr), 14th - sugar (49.7 kg/capita/yr), 18th - fish (40.4 kg/capita/yr), 20th - stimulants (9.0 kg/capita/yr), 25th - spices (2.7 kg/capita/yr), 27th - meat (82.8 kg/capita/yr), 44th - treenuts (3.4 kg/capita/yr), 81st - fruits (81.5 kg/capita/yr), 83rd - cereals (133.4 kg/capita/yr), 86th - vegetable oils (10.6 kg/capita/yr), 95th - vegetables (65.4 kg/capita/yr), 104th - milk (70.0 kg/capita/yr), 134th - alcoholic beverages (10.8 kg/capita/yr), 146th - starchy roots (22.9 kg/capita/yr), 150th - pulses (1.2 kg/capita/yr).

Part V. Reproduction

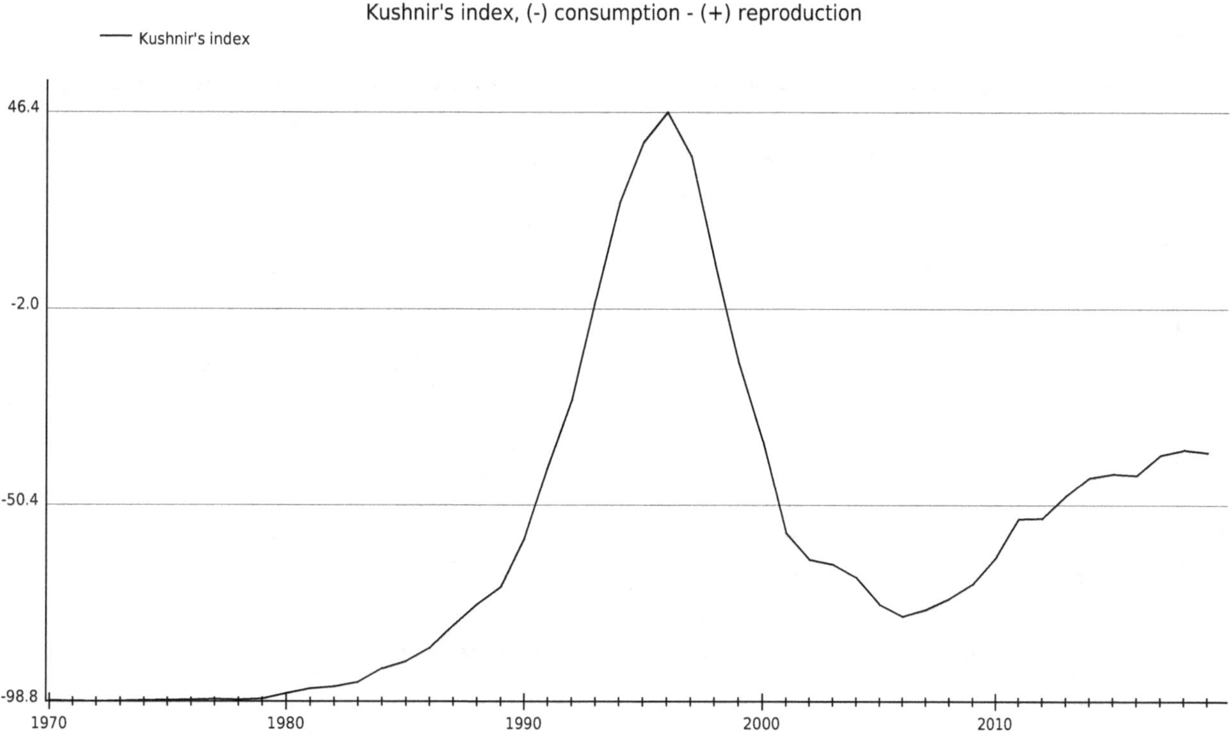

Chapter XV. Gross fixed capital formation

(including Acquisitions less disposals of valuables)

The Brunei's fixed capital formation grew from $61.1 million per year in the 1970s to $4.9 billion per year in the 2010s, that is by $4.9 billion or 80.9 times. The change occurred at $4.4 billion due to a 8.7-fold increase in prices, as also at $409.1 million due to a 3.6-fold increase in per capita rate, as well as at $97.7 million due to the growth in population. The average annual growth in gross fixed capital formation is 6.1%. The minimum value of gross fixed capital formation was in 1970 at $8.8 million. The maximum value of fixed capital formation was in 2013 at $7.1 billion.

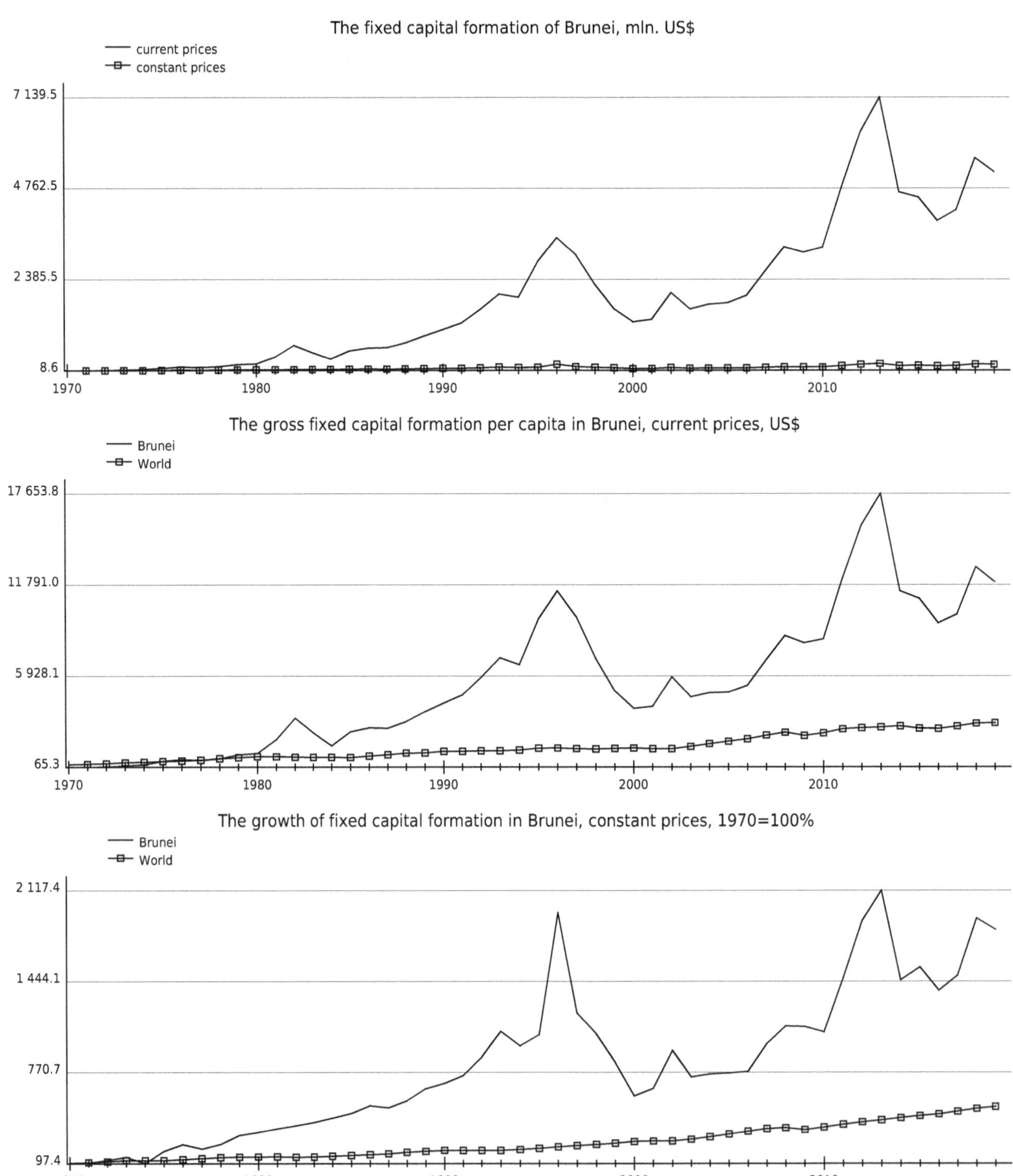

The fixed capital formation of Brunei, mln. US$

The gross fixed capital formation per capita in Brunei, current prices, US$

The growth of fixed capital formation in Brunei, constant prices, 1970=100%

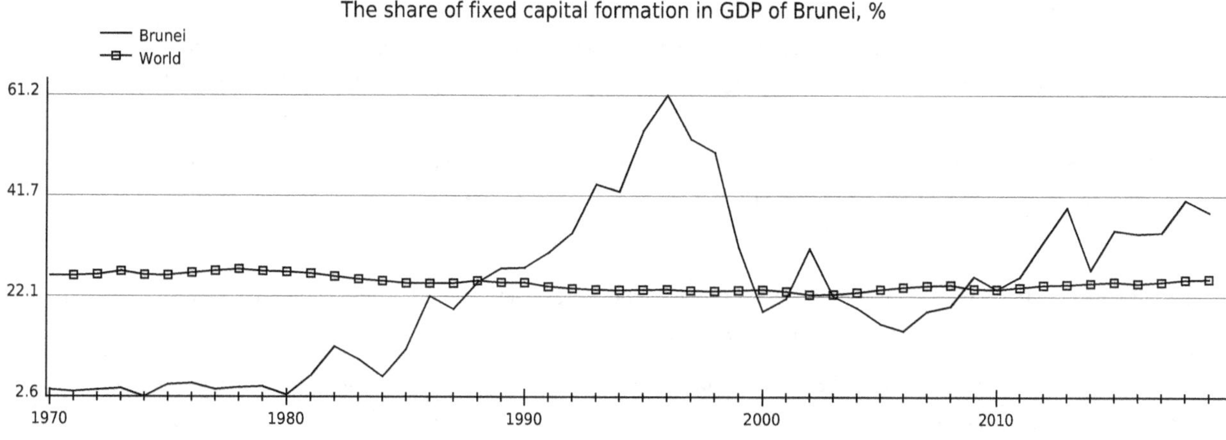

The 1970s

The Brunei's gross fixed capital formation was $61.1 million per year in the 1970s, ranked 147th in the world, and was on a par with Rwanda ($59.9 million). The share in the world was 0.0035%, and 0.017% in Asia.

The share of gross fixed capital formation in GDP of Brunei was 4.3% in the 1970s, ranked 183rd in the world.

The Brunei's gross fixed capital formation per capita was $385.6 in the 1970s, ranked 65th in the world, and was on a par with South Africa ($385.1), the Virgin Islands ($392.4), Mauritania ($393.1). The Brunei's gross fixed capital formation per capita was less than fixed capital formation per capita in the world ($433.5) by 11.0%, and was greater than gross fixed capital formation per capita in Asia ($151.1) in 2.6 times.

The growth of fixed capital formation in Brunei was 13.2% in the 1970s, ranked 27th in the world. The growth of gross fixed capital formation in Brunei (13.2%) was greater than growth of fixed capital formation in the world (4.2%), was greater than growth of gross fixed capital formation in Asia (6.2%).

Comparison with neighbors. The Brunei's gross fixed capital formation was less than in Malaysia ($2.4 billion). The fixed capital formation per capita in Brunei was greater than in Malaysia ($201.4). The growth of gross fixed capital formation in Brunei was less than in Malaysia (15.2%).

Comparison with leaders. The Brunei's fixed capital formation was less than in the USA ($381.9 billion), in the USSR ($214.6 billion), in Japan ($191.6 billion), in Germany ($125.8 billion), and in France ($82.9 billion). The gross fixed capital formation per capita in Brunei was less than in the USA ($1 750.0), in Japan ($1 720.7), in Germany ($1 597.2), in France ($1 545.4), and in the USSR ($850.9). The growth of gross fixed capital formation in Brunei was greater than in the United States (4.4%), in Japan (3.9%), in the USSR (3.2%), in France (2.7%), and in Germany (1.5%).

The 1980s

The Brunei's fixed capital formation was $537.8 million per year in the 1980s, ranked 105th in the world, and was on a par with Vietnam ($525.2 million). The share in the world was 0.014%, and 0.054% in Asia.

The share of fixed capital formation in GDP of Brunei was 12.5% in the 1980s, ranked 169th in the world, and was on a par with Vietnam (12.5%), Puerto Rico (12.5%).

The fixed capital formation per capita in Brunei was $2 423.7 in the 1980s, ranked 31st in the world, and was on a par with Belgium ($2.5 thousand), Italy ($2.4 thousand). The Brunei's fixed capital formation per capita was greater than gross fixed capital formation per capita in the world ($790.9) in 3.1 times, and was greater than gross fixed capital formation per capita in Asia ($349.2) in 6.9 times.

The growth of fixed capital formation in Brunei was 7.8% in the 1980s, ranked 21st in the world. The growth of fixed capital formation in Brunei (7.8%) was greater than growth of gross fixed capital formation in the world (2.5%), was greater than growth of fixed capital formation in Asia (4.8%).

Comparison with neighbors. The Brunei's gross fixed capital formation was less than in Malaysia ($9.2 billion). The gross fixed capital formation per capita in Brunei was greater than in Malaysia ($591.5). The growth of gross fixed capital formation in Brunei was greater than in Malaysia (6.6%).

Comparison with leaders. The fixed capital formation of Brunei was less than in the United States ($958.4 billion), in Japan ($571.7 billion), in the USSR ($271.0 billion), in Germany ($238.1 billion), and in France ($164.3 billion). The Brunei's fixed capital formation per capita was greater than in the USSR ($984.8); but less than in Japan ($4.7 thousand), in the United States ($4.0 thousand), in Germany ($3.1 thousand), and in France ($2.9 thousand). The growth of gross fixed capital formation in Brunei was greater than in Japan (4.8%), in the United States (3.1%), in France (2.4%), in the USSR (1.7%), and in Germany (1.4%).

The 1990s

The fixed capital formation of Brunei was $2.1 billion per year in the 1990s, ranked 85th in the world, and was on a par with Cameroon ($2.1 billion), Costa Rica ($2.1 billion). The share in the world was 0.031%, and 0.092% in Asia.

The share of fixed capital formation in GDP of Brunei was 43.9% in the 1990s, ranked 5th in the world, and was on a par with São Tomé and Príncipe (43.6%), Montserrat (43.5%).

The gross fixed capital formation per capita in Brunei was $7 194.6 in the 1990s, ranked 10th in the world, and was on a par with Norway ($7.3 thousand). The Brunei's gross fixed capital formation per capita was greater than fixed capital formation per capita in the world ($1 183.8) in 6.1 times, and was greater than gross fixed capital formation per capita in Asia ($661.5) in 10.9 times.

The growth of fixed capital formation in Brunei was 2.7% in the 1990s, ranked 117th in the world, and was on a par with Burkina Faso (2.6%), Northern Africa (2.6%), Jordan (2.6%). The growth of fixed capital formation in Brunei (2.7%) was less than growth of fixed capital formation in the world (2.8%), was less than growth of gross fixed capital formation in Asia (4.3%).

Comparison with neighbors. The Brunei's gross fixed capital formation was less than in Malaysia ($27.2 billion). The gross fixed capital formation per capita in Brunei was greater than in Malaysia ($1 338.4). The growth of gross fixed capital formation in Brunei was less than in Malaysia (6.2%).

Comparison with leaders. The Brunei's fixed capital formation was less than in the United States ($1.6 trillion), in Japan ($1.3 trillion), in Germany ($520.7 billion), in France ($299.3 billion), and in the United Kingdom ($250.0 billion). The fixed capital formation per capita in Brunei was greater than in Germany ($6.5 thousand), in the United States ($6.1 thousand), in France ($5.0 thousand), and in the United Kingdom ($4.3 thousand); but less than in Japan ($10.4 thousand). The growth of fixed capital formation in Brunei was greater than in Germany (2.4%), in the UK (1.7%), in France (1.5%), and in Japan (0.18%); but less than in the United States (4.8%).

The 2000s

The gross fixed capital formation of Brunei was $2.1 billion per year in the 2000s, ranked 117th in the world. The share in the world was 0.019%, and 0.058% in Asia.

The share of fixed capital formation in GDP of Brunei was 20.7% in the 2000s, ranked 147th in the world, and was on a par with Gambia (20.7%), Malta (20.6%), Liberia (20.6%).

The gross fixed capital formation per capita in Brunei was $5 739.9 in the 2000s, ranked 39th in the world, and was on a par with Cyprus ($5.7 thousand). The fixed capital formation per capita in Brunei was greater than gross fixed capital formation per capita in the world ($1 690.7) in 3.4 times, and was greater than fixed capital formation per capita in Asia ($905.5) in 6.3 times.

The growth of gross fixed capital formation in Brunei was 2.8% in the 2000s, ranked 129th in the world. The growth of gross fixed capital formation in Brunei (2.8%) was less than growth of gross fixed capital formation in the world (3.5%), was less than growth of fixed capital formation in Asia (6.8%).

Comparison with neighbors. The gross fixed capital formation of Brunei was less than in Malaysia ($32.5 billion). The gross fixed capital formation per capita in Brunei was greater than in Malaysia ($1 274.9). The growth of gross fixed capital formation in Brunei was less than in Malaysia (4.9%).

Comparison with leaders. The gross fixed capital formation of Brunei was less than in the United States ($2.8 trillion), in Japan ($1.2 trillion), in China ($1.0 trillion), in Germany ($557.7 billion), and in France ($463.9 billion). The gross fixed capital formation per capita in Brunei was greater than in China ($782.2); but less than in the USA ($9.4 thousand), in Japan ($9.0 thousand), in France ($7.4 thousand), and in Germany ($6.9 thousand). The growth of fixed capital formation in Brunei was greater than in France (1.6%), in the USA (0.43%), in Germany (-0.56%), and in Japan (-2.0%); but less than in China (13.4%).

The 2010s

The Brunei's gross fixed capital formation was $4.9 billion per year in the 2010s, ranked 108th in the world, and was on a par with Mozambique ($4.9 billion), Equatorial Guinea ($4.9 billion), Botswana ($5.1 billion). The share in the world was 0.026%, and 0.056% in Asia.

The share of fixed capital formation in GDP of Brunei was 33.0% in the 2010s, ranked 20th in the world, and was on a par with Mongolia (32.7%).

The fixed capital formation per capita in Brunei was $12 010.8 in the 2010s, ranked 15th in the world, and was on a par with Denmark ($11.9 thousand). The gross fixed capital formation per capita in Brunei was greater than fixed capital formation per capita in the world ($2 621.1) in 4.6 times, and was greater than fixed capital formation per capita in Asia ($2 007.4) in 6.0 times.

The growth of gross fixed capital formation in Brunei was 5.1% in the 2010s, ranked 71st in the world, and was on a par with Montenegro (5.1%). The growth of fixed capital formation in Brunei (5.1%) was greater than growth of fixed capital formation in the world (4.1%), was less than growth of gross fixed capital formation in Asia (6.0%).

Comparison with neighbors. The gross fixed capital formation of Brunei was 15.8 times lower than in Malaysia ($78.2 billion). The gross fixed capital formation per capita in Brunei was 4.6 times higher than in Malaysia ($2.6 thousand). The growth of fixed capital formation in Brunei was less than in Malaysia (6.0%).

Comparison with leaders. The gross fixed capital formation of Brunei was 914.6 times lower than in China ($4.5 trillion), 727.8 times lower than in the United States ($3.6 trillion), 244.7 times lower than in Japan ($1.2 trillion), 152.2 times lower than in Germany ($752.5 billion), and 140.9 times lower than in India ($696.8 billion). The Brunei's gross fixed capital formation per capita was 6.6% higher than in the USA ($11.3 thousand), 27.0% higher than in Japan ($9.5 thousand), 30.7% higher than in Germany ($9.2 thousand), 3.7 times higher than in China ($3.2 thousand), and 22.4 times higher than in India ($535.2). The growth of gross fixed capital formation in Brunei was greater than in the United States (3.8%), in Germany (2.8%), and in Japan (1.8%); but less than in China (8.0%) and in India (5.8%).